Smithsonian Treasures *of* American History

Smithsonian

Treasures *of*

American

History

Kathleen M. Kendrick
Peter C. Liebhold

Published in association with the National Museum of American History
Kenneth E. Behring Center

Smithsonian Books

Collins
An Imprint of HarperCollins Publishers

Except where otherwise noted, all photographs
are copyright Smithsonian Institution.

Photographer credits: Richard Strauss, Hugh Talman,
Harold Dorwin, Chrissy Walker, Tyler Northrup.

HarperCollins books may be purchased for educational, business, or sales
promotional use. For information please write: Special Markets Department,
HarperCollins Publishers, 10 East 53rd Street, New York, NY 10022.

First Smithsonian Books edition published 2006.

Designed by Timothy Shaner

The Library of Congress Cataloging-in-Publication Data has been applied for.

ISBN-10: 0-06-117103-4
ISBN-13: 978-0-06-117103-1

06 07 08 09 10 ❖/RRD 9 8 7 6 5 4 3 2 1

CONTENTS

TREASURES OF AMERICAN HISTORY

The Smithsonian's National Museum of American History preserves treasures of the American past. From politics to popular culture, innovations to everyday life, the Museum's collections reflect the diverse experiences, beliefs, and dreams that have shaped the nation. For millions of visitors who come to Washington every year, the Museum provides unique opportunities to connect with history through objects that have been cherished, preserved, and passed down by generations of Americans.

Within this book, you will encounter some of the most important and prized treasures of the National Museum of American History. Selected from more than three million artifacts in the Museum's collections, they include a mix of the famous and the familiar, the unexpected and the extraordinary. All have compelling stories to tell, and each offers its own valuable connection to a shared American past.

In "Creativity & Innovation," we present treasures of scientific discovery, technological invention, and artistic creation. From the first complete artificial heart implanted in a human being to the first bottles of California wine to win a Paris tasting, these objects evoke the innovative American spirit in varied and sometimes provocative ways.

Treasures of "American Biography" honor the lives and accomplishments of celebrated individuals. Some of these objects, like Albert Einstein's briar pipe and Marilyn Monroe's kidskin gloves, represent traits of character and personality. Others, like Louis Armstrong's childhood cornet, signify obstacles overcome on the path to achievement.

"National Challenges" defines another kind of treasure, objects associated with critical moments in the social and political development of the United States. From the desk on which Thomas Jefferson drafted the Declaration of Independence to a lunch counter where students sat to protest racial segregation in Greensboro, North Carolina, these treasures mark historic and con-

INTRODUCTION

tinuing struggles to define, extend, and uphold the nation's founding ideals of freedom and equality.

The final chapter, "American Identity," explores the diverse cultural traditions of the American people. These treasures suggest the many ways Americans have expressed their heritage and values—such as through faith, as in a sun stone from the Mormon temple at Nauvoo, Illinois, or through music, as in the piano used by Irving Berlin to compose some of his greatest popular hits. Together, these objects encourage us to contemplate what it means to be American.

The National Museum of American History is only the keeper of these treasures, which, along with all the Smithsonian's vast collections, belong to the American people. But by preserving these objects and sharing their stories, the Museum seeks to help Americans realize the value of their heritage and ensure that the treasures of the past will continue to inspire future generations.

Brent D. Glass
Director, National Museum of American History

CREATIVITY & INNOVATION

S ince its inception, the United States has defined itself as an innovative nation, and the National Museum of American History has documented this creative spirit in its many forms. From science and industry to the arts, a dynamic interaction of ideas, traditions, and talents has fueled new achievements and influenced the national experience.

Innovation has been inspired by complex and varied motivations—and it has also come with unintended consequences.

Edison Light Bulb, 1879

A technological breakthrough that has become a symbol for innovative ideas, this carbon-filament electric light bulb was invented by Thomas Edison and unveiled to the public at his Menlo Park laboratory on New Year's Eve, 1879.

As the quintessential American inventor-hero, Edison personified the ideal of the hardworking self-made man. He received a record 1,093 patents and became a skilled entrepreneur. Though occasionally unsuccessful, Edison and his team developed many practical devices in his "invention factory," and fostered faith in technological progress.

Opposite: Thomas Edison (1847–1931) (*Library of Congress*)

Dorothy's Ruby Slippers, 1938

These sequined shoes were worn by 16-year-old Judy Garland as Dorothy in *The Wizard of Oz*.

In the original book by L. Frank Baum, Dorothy's magic slippers are silver; for the Technicolor movie, they were changed to ruby red to show up more vividly against the yellow-brick road. One of several pairs used during filming, these size-five shoes are well-worn, suggesting they were Garland's primary pair for dancing scenes.

Script for *The Wizard of Oz*, 1938

The challenge of adapting L. Frank Baum's book to film began with the screenplay. From March 1938 to March 1939, more than a dozen people, most uncredited, worked on writing and revising the script.

This page, from an early version of the script by lead screenwriter Noel Langley, notes the change from black and white to color. In this famous scene, Dorothy steps out of her farmhouse into Oz and says to her dog, Toto, "I've got a feeling we're not in Kansas anymore."

23

94

CLOSE UP - DOROTHY

with her eyes tight shut. Toto has his
head tucked well under her arm. Slowly she
opens her eyes.

FULL SHOT - ROOM -

All four legs of the bed are spread-eagled on
the floor and the furniture has been jerked
out of place. A chair or two lie on their
backs. There is dead silence on the SOUND
TRACK as Dorothy gets off the bed and tip
toes to the door.

WIPE TO:

MED. SHOT - INT. FRONT DOOR

Dorothy opens the door slowly and peers out.

FULL SHOT - MUNCHKIN COUNTRY - (First full colour shot.)

quite empty of all sign of life. The only
sound is the twittering of a bird or two in
the distance.

MED. SHOT - DOOR - EXT.

Dorothy comes cautiously out, with Toto under
her arm, and looks about. Music comes up
softly.

Dorothy (after a pause)
I've got a feeling we're not in Kansas any more.

For generations, this 1939 MGM fantasy musical has held a cherished place in American popular culture. Based on the classic children's book by L. Frank Baum, it tells the story of Dorothy Gale, a Kansas farm girl transported to the magical Land of Oz. With its dazzling special effects, costumes, and sets rendered in vibrant Technicolor, The Wizard of Oz represents one of the all-time greatest achievements in movie magic.

Scarecrow Costume, 1938

Ray Bolger wore this patchwork outfit as the Scarecrow, one of the trio of friends who accompany Dorothy to the Emerald City in The Wizard of Oz.

Designed by Adrian, MGM's premier costume artist, the straw-stuffed clothing fit loosely enough so that Bolger could perform his comedic dance number, "If I Only Had a Brain." A sponge-rubber mask, resembling burlap, completed the Scarecrow's costume. Under the hot lights on the set, the mask was stifling, and it frequently had to be replaced.

Technicolor Camera, around 1938

In The Wizard of Oz, Dorothy's journey from Kansas to Oz is symbolized by a shift from black and white to Technicolor. This camera was one of several used to film the Oz scenes.

Invented in 1932, the Technicolor camera recorded on three separate negatives—red, blue, and green—which were then combined to develop a full-color positive print. The box encasing the camera, called a "blimp," muffled the machine's sound during filming.

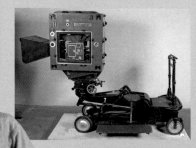

THE BIRTH OF TELECOMMUNICATION

Long before cell phones and the Internet, the first worldwide telecommunications web emerged in the 1800s with the invention of the telegraph and the telephone. By delivering information at the speed of electricity over wires that gradually stretched across the country and around the globe, these innovations created a network of opportunities for a rapidly expanding society.

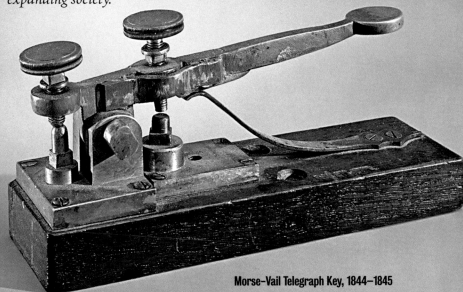

Morse-Vail Telegraph Key, 1844–1845

This key, believed to be from the first American telegraph line, was built by Alfred Vail as an improvement on Samuel Morse's original transmitter. Vail helped Morse develop a practical system for sending and receiving coded electrical signals over a wire, which was successfully demonstrated in 1844.

Morse's telegraph marked the arrival of instant long-distance communication in America. The revolutionary technology excited the public imagination, inspiring predictions that the telegraph would bring about economic prosperity, national unity, and even world peace.

Telegraph Message, 1844

Printed in Morse code and transcribed by Samuel Morse himself, this message was transmitted from Baltimore to Washington, D.C., over the nation's first long-distance telegraph line.

In 1843, Congress allocated $30,000 for Morse to build an electric telegraph line between Washington and Baltimore. Morse and his partner, Alfred Vail, completed the 40-mile line in May 1844. For the first transmissions, they used a quotation from the Bible, Numbers 23:23: "What hath God wrought!"

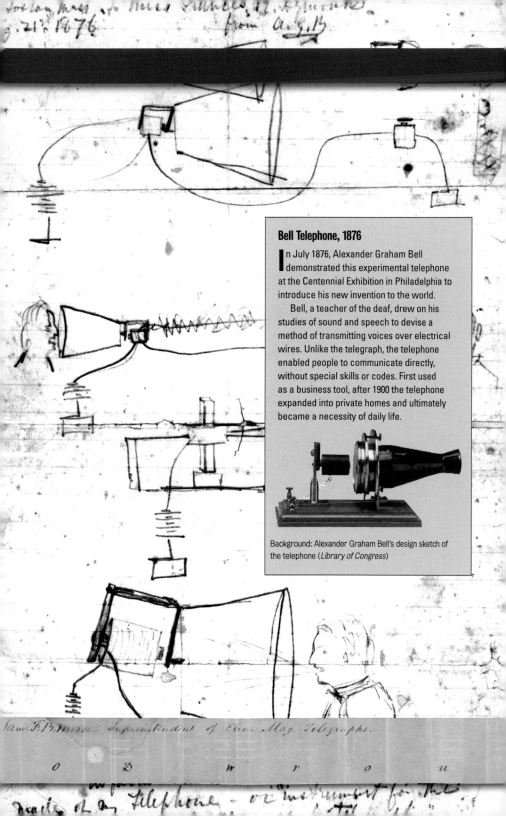

Bell Telephone, 1876

In July 1876, Alexander Graham Bell demonstrated this experimental telephone at the Centennial Exhibition in Philadelphia to introduce his new invention to the world.

Bell, a teacher of the deaf, drew on his studies of sound and speech to devise a method of transmitting voices over electrical wires. Unlike the telegraph, the telephone enabled people to communicate directly, without special skills or codes. First used as a business tool, after 1900 the telephone expanded into private homes and ultimately became a necessity of daily life.

Background: Alexander Graham Bell's design sketch of the telephone (*Library of Congress*)

HUMAN MACHINES

Since the 19th century, inventors have designed increasingly complex, automated machines to supplement, enhance, and even replace human activities. While many welcomed mechanization as a labor-saving and even life-saving boon, others expressed fears of a world of mechanical droids or of being supplanted by automation.

Liotta–Cooley Artificial Heart, 1969

The first total artificial heart implanted in a human, this device was developed by Domingo Liotta and implanted by surgeon Denton Cooley on April 4, 1969. The recipient, Haskell Karp, lived for 64 hours with the artificial heart until a human heart was available for transplant.

Although Karp died soon after receiving a real heart, the procedure demonstrated the viability of artificial hearts as a bridge to transplant in cardiac patients. However, some criticized the surgery as unethical because it was performed without formal review by the medical community.

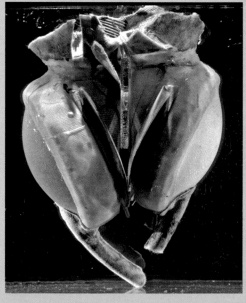

Left: Artificial heart patient Haskell Karp at St. Luke's Episcopal Hospital, Houston, Texas, 1969. After the artificial heart was implanted, it took a battery of machines to keep him alive.

Gilbreth Stopwatch, 1910–1920

Efficiency experts Frank and Lillian Gilbreth took time-lapse photographs and used customized watches and clocks in an attempt to find "the one best way" to do the job.

The Gilbreths were pioneers of the early 20th-century movement known as scientific management. By separating "thinking" from "doing" and reducing jobs to a series of physical repetitions, scientific managers hoped to maximize efficiency, increase productivity, and boost corporate profits. Workers, however, feared they were being turned into machines.

Background: Time-lapse photograph of a woman assembling buttons, 1917. Frank and Lillian Gilbreth made this worker's movements visible by attaching lights to her hands and head and photographing her in dim light with a long exposure.

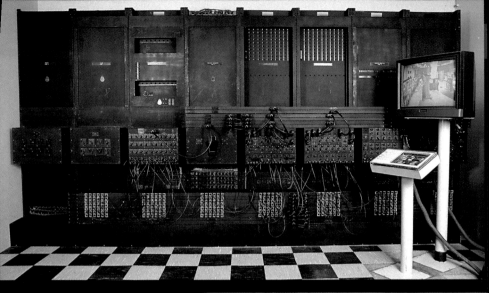

ENIAC, 1942

The machine that launched the computer industry, ENIAC (Electronic Numerical Integrator and Computer) was developed during World War II to compute artillery range tables. This is only a small portion of ENIAC, which altogether took up 1,500 square feet of space, weighed 30 tons, and contained 18,000 vacuum tubes.

While ENIAC could function much faster than the human brain, its capability was still lower than a modern scientific calculator. It also required a large staff of tube-changers, programmers, and operators to keep it running.

Horn & Hardart Automat, 1902

In 1902, Joseph Horn and Frank Hardart opened their first "waiterless restaurant" in Philadelphia. With its bank of glass-fronted, coin-operated vending machines, the Automat offered an irresistible combination of cheap food, quick service, and technological novelty. Of course, the Automat was not totally automated; as customers emptied the food compartments, the slots were refilled by staff hidden behind the machine.

A 35-foot section of the Automat, collected by the Smithsonian after the restaurant closed in 1960s, features the original decorative framework with later vending apparatus.

Above: ENIAC in use at the Ballistic Research Laboratory, Aberdeen, Maryland, 1948. Most of the early operations were handled by women.

Above: Customers make their purchases from the first Automat located on Chestnut Street in Philadelphia, Pennsylvania.

R2-D2 and C-3PO, from *Return of the Jedi*, about 1982

Created by *Star Wars* filmmaker George Lucas, these two "droids" are among the most famous of all science-fiction robots. The little R2-D2 is spunky and resourceful, while his companion, the more human-looking C-3PO, is a bit of a worrywart. Of course, both of these robots were really costumes with an actor inside.

Human-like robots have long been a staple of popular culture, depicted in both positive and menacing ways. In reality, while engineers have made great strides in practical robotics and artificial intelligence, real robots seldom appear in human form.

REINVENTING DAILY LIFE

Imagine if you had never before ridden a bicycle, snapped a photo, or worn a pair of jeans. These experiences, so much a part of daily life today, were once technological novelties. While the original versions may look peculiar compared to their modern-day descendants, they provide fascinating early glimpses of innovations that influenced how Americans lived, worked, and played.

Crayola Crayons, around 1903

Cherished by generations of child artists, Crayola crayons were invented in 1903 by the Binney & Smith Company of Easton, Pennsylvania. Using paraffin wax and nontoxic pigments, the company produced a coloring stick that was safe, sturdy, and affordable. The name Crayola, coined by the wife of the company's founder, comes from "craie," French for chalk, and "oleaginous," or oily.

This Crayola set for "young artists" was one of the earliest produced. Its 28 colors included celestial blue, golden ochre, rose pink, and burnt sienna.

Levi Strauss Jeans, 1875–1896

Though made of brown duck rather than blue denim, these "Levi's"—one of the oldest known pairs—feature the familiar riveted pockets, button fly, and waistband patch of modern jeans.

In 1873, San Francisco merchant Levi Strauss and tailor Jacob Davis patented a design for workers' trousers reinforced by copper rivets. Strauss manufactured the pants from cheap, sturdy fabrics, including a cotton material called "jean." Initially worn by miners and cowboys, jeans evolved into casual clothing for all ages, classes, and lifestyles.

Swanson's TV Dinner Tray, 1955

Made of shiny aluminum with three compartments for meat, vegetable, and whipped potatoes, this early TV Dinner tray symbolized a square meal for the television age.

Introduced by C. A. Swanson & Sons in 1953, the frozen, precooked TV Dinner could be heated and ready to eat in 25 minutes. The meals were named to emphasize their modern, convenient design—as easy to prepare as turning on a television set. Portable and self-contained, TV Dinners also made it easier for 1950s families to combine dinner with their new favorite pastime.

Swanson's TV Dinner advertisement, 1958

Terry Box Clock, 1816

Before Eli Terry invented this simple shelf clock, only the wealthy could afford to have a timepiece in their homes.

In his Connecticut factory, Terry mass-produced clocks from interchangeable wooden parts, a technique known as the "American system." Machine-made clocks added to the abundance of cheap consumer goods generated during the Industrial Revolution, and soon they became a staple of the average American household. Even those who did not know how to tell time bought clocks as decorative objects for their mantels.

Draisine (Early Bicycle), around 1818

One of the oldest surviving ancestors of the modern bicycle, this wooden two-wheeler is named for its German inventor, Baron von Drais.

Also known as a velocipede or hobby horse, the draisine enjoyed brief popularity in Europe and the United States during the 1810s and 1820s. To propel the machine, riders pushed along the ground with their feet. In 1863 a new invention, the pedal, helped transform the bicycle into a more practical and widespread mode of transportation.

Kodak Camera, 1888

This original Kodak camera, introduced by George Eastman, placed the power of photography in the hands of anyone who could press a button.

Unlike earlier cameras that used a glass-plate negative for each exposure, the Kodak came pre-loaded with a 100-exposure roll of flexible film. After finishing the roll, the consumer mailed the camera back to the factory to have the prints made. In capturing everyday moments and memories, the Kodak's distinctive circular snapshots defined a new style of photography—informal, personal, and fun.

Above: Early Kodak snapshot of a family looking at Kodak pictures. Left: Kodak advertisement, 1891.

NEW KODAKS

"You press the button, we do the rest."

Seven new Styles and Sizes
ALL LOADED WITH Transparent Films.
For sale by all Photo. Stock Dealers.
THE EASTMAN COMPANY,
ROCHESTER, N. Y.

Send for Catalogue.

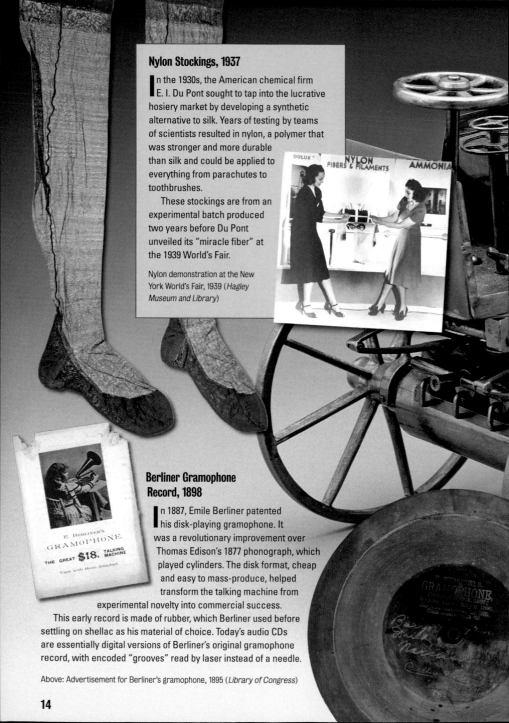

Nylon Stockings, 1937

In the 1930s, the American chemical firm E. I. Du Pont sought to tap into the lucrative hosiery market by developing a synthetic alternative to silk. Years of testing by teams of scientists resulted in nylon, a polymer that was stronger and more durable than silk and could be applied to everything from parachutes to toothbrushes.

These stockings are from an experimental batch produced two years before Du Pont unveiled its "miracle fiber" at the 1939 World's Fair.

Nylon demonstration at the New York World's Fair, 1939 (*Hagley Museum and Library*)

Berliner Gramophone Record, 1898

In 1887, Emile Berliner patented his disk-playing gramophone. It was a revolutionary improvement over Thomas Edison's 1877 phonograph, which played cylinders. The disk format, cheap and easy to mass-produce, helped transform the talking machine from experimental novelty into commercial success.

This early record is made of rubber, which Berliner used before settling on shellac as his material of choice. Today's audio CDs are essentially digital versions of Berliner's original gramophone record, with encoded "grooves" read by laser instead of a needle.

Above: Advertisement for Berliner's gramophone, 1895 (*Library of Congress*)

14

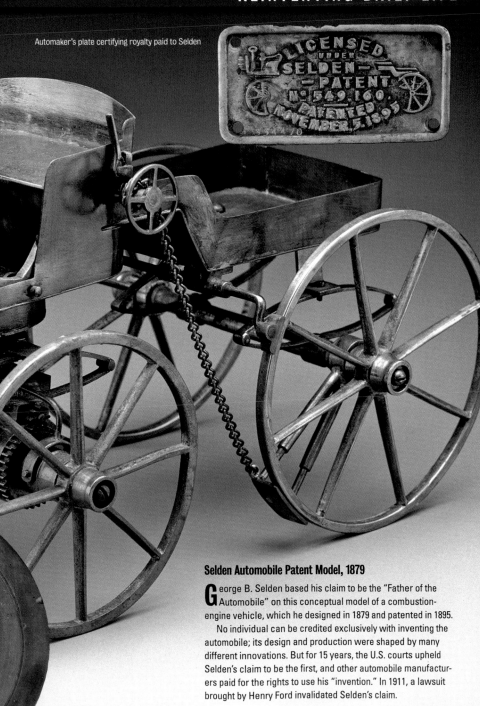

Automaker's plate certifying royalty paid to Selden

LICENSED UNDER SELDEN PATENT No. 549.160. PATENTED NOVEMBER 5. 1895

Selden Automobile Patent Model, 1879

George B. Selden based his claim to be the "Father of the Automobile" on this conceptual model of a combustion-engine vehicle, which he designed in 1879 and patented in 1895.

No individual can be credited exclusively with inventing the automobile; its design and production were shaped by many different innovations. But for 15 years, the U.S. courts upheld Selden's claim to be the first, and other automobile manufacturers paid for the rights to use his "invention." In 1911, a lawsuit brought by Henry Ford invalidated Selden's claim.

Horned Grebe, by John J. Audubon, 1835

Paired with the copper plate from which it was printed, this large, exquisitely detailed engraving is from John J. Audubon's ornithological masterpiece, *Birds of America.*

Through this work, a total of 435 prints published over eleven years, Audubon introduced new ways of looking at wildlife. Instead of depicting birds as scientific specimens, he painted them as living creatures, life-size, in realistic settings and poses. Audubon's images contributed to later public interest in wildlife conservation.

$20 Pattern Coin by Augustus Saint-Gaudens, 1907

In 1905, President Theodore Roosevelt enlisted sculptor Augustus Saint-Gaudens to beautify the nation's coinage. His $20 piece, or "double eagle," is one of the most stunning and valuable U.S. coins ever made. Featuring a majestic figure of Liberty striding out of the dawn, it transcends its monetary function as a bold and imaginative work of art.

Less than two dozen of these extraordinary coins were minted. The ultra-high-relief design, inspired by ancient Greek coins, proved impractical to produce, so it was flattened for mass circulation.

Reverse side of coin

Tiffany Floor Lamp, around 1900

In designing his celebrated stained-glass pieces, Louis Comfort Tiffany often took inspiration from nature, and this bamboo-style lamp is a magnificent example.

From the graceful bronze base molded like a stalk to the seedpod finial on top, the lamp conveys its organic motif through form, color, and texture. Artisans in Tiffany's studio carefully selected each piece of greenish yellow glass to achieve the effect of sun-dappled leaves on the illuminated shade.

"Minerva" Dress, by Oscar de la Renta, 2002

This gilded evening dress expresses the flair for elegance, drama, and luxury that has made Oscar de la Renta one of the most acclaimed American fashion designers.

Designed for the French couture firm Pierre Balmain, the ensemble features a silk top adorned with overlapping rows of gold-painted feathers and a skirt of pleated gold lamé. Alluding to its divine qualities, de la Renta named his creation after Minerva, the Roman goddess of wisdom.

Stradivarius Violin, the "Greffuhle," about 1709

Handcrafted by Antonio Stradivari in Cremona, Italy, this instrument represents an artistic standard of perfection recognized by classical musicians in the United States and around the world.

Of the 620 Stradivarius instruments that survive, this is one of only eleven that are decorated. The inlay along the sides—an ornate motif of flowers, vines, and animals—suggests symbolic representation of eternal life and the promise of paradise. The brilliant tone of the Greffuhle (named for a French nobleman who once owned it) can still be heard today in concerts by the Smithsonian's Axelrod String Quartet.

Manuscript of *A Love Supreme* by John Coltrane, 1964

A musical revelation captured on paper, this is the original sketch for John Coltrane's 33-minute jazz masterpiece, *A Love Supreme*.

One of the most innovative and emulated saxophonists in jazz history, Coltrane communicated through his music on intellectual, emotional, and spiritual levels. *A Love Supreme* was inspired by a religious awakening he experienced after overcoming drug addiction. In a suite of four parts—"Acknowledgement," "Resolution," "Pursuance," and "Psalm"—it offers complex and impassioned reflections on prayer, faith, and the search for inner peace.

Above: John Coltrane, 1957

1973 Chateau Montelena Chardonnay, made by Miljenko Grgich (Left)
1973 Stag's Leap Wine Cellars Cabernet Sauvignon, made by Warren Winiarski (Right)

In 1976 these two American vintages placed first in an international competition, challenging the conventional belief that fine wine could only come from France.

The 1976 Paris tasting, judged by nine of France's leading wine experts, pitted California reds and whites against their French counterparts in a blind test. The unexpected victory established California's Napa Valley as a premier winemaking region and launched the expansion of wine production in the United States.

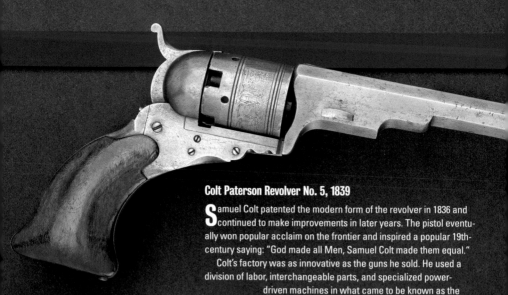

Colt Paterson Revolver No. 5, 1839

Samuel Colt patented the modern form of the revolver in 1836 and continued to make improvements in later years. The pistol eventually won popular acclaim on the frontier and inspired a popular 19th-century saying: "God made all Men, Samuel Colt made them equal."

Colt's factory was as innovative as the guns he sold. He used a division of labor, interchangeable parts, and specialized power-driven machines in what came to be known as the "American system" of production.

Hart Parr #3 Tractor, 1903

This 14,000-pound behemoth is the oldest surviving internal combustion tractor in the United States. The Hart Parr company of Charles City, Iowa, first coined the word "tractor" in 1903 to describe its invention.

In the 19th century, farmers relied on horse-drawn equipment and mobile steam-powered traction engines for harvesting and threshing. The internal combustion tractor, which could power an array of farm machinery, greatly reduced the manpower and skill required to operate "factories in the fields."

Machine for Making Paper Bags, 1879

This machine for making paper bags was invented by Margaret Knight, of Massachusetts. She patented numerous inventions, from factory machinery to household improvements, leading some to celebrate her as a "female Edison."

While many women had innovative ideas, 19th-century societal norms and a patent system that favored male inventors made it difficult for women to secure patents under their own names. Knight's patent is widely celebrated because it demonstrates women's participation in the important American process of invention.

Innovation has been celebrated in the United States for creating national well-being and exemplifying personal achievement. For some people, invention was a means for obtaining individual wealth; for others it was a strategy for solving technical problems or dealing with labor issues. The ultimate effect of new technology is often hard to predict. Inventions sometimes increase productivity, lower costs, and increase consumer choice. Other times there are unanticipated consequences that can create social and economic upheaval.

Sholes & Glidden Typewriter, 1874

The first commercially successful American writing machine, this typewriter was manufactured by E. Remington and Sons from a design patented by Christopher Sholes and Carlos Glidden. The keys were specially arranged to prevent them from jamming and promote faster typing, creating the "QWERTY" keyboard still used today.

As the nature of office work changed in the late 19th century, the introduction of the typewriter created new job opportunities for women. Unlike the male clerks whom they replaced, however, female office workers had far fewer chances for advancement.

John Bull Steam Locomotive, 1831

The *John Bull* was one of the first successful locomotives in the United States. Imported from England in 1831, it was significantly altered to meet the conditions of American railroads. By the end of the 1830s American manufacturers had made many innovative design improvements and were exporting locomotives.

Railroads mechanized transportation, facilitating the movement of goods over long distances. Perhaps of greater importance was the creation of management techniques needed to operate the complex railroad system.

Harvester and Self-Raking Reaper, 1877

William Whiteley of Springfield, Ohio, submitted this unusually decorative model along with his patent application.
The Museum's holding of about 10,000 patent models (originally submitted to the Patent Office in the 19th century) is a prized treasure of the collection. While most inventions, like Whiteley's reaper, are simple incremental improvements, the models illustrate the dreams of individuals who hoped to advance American industry, make their fortunes, prove their genius, and demonstrate their value to society.

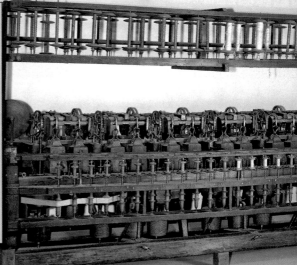

Slater Spinning Frame, 1790

This machine for making yarn was built under the direction of Samuel Slater at the dawn of the Industrial Revolution. The technology was not invented in the United States but "borrowed" by Slater as he emigrated from England. A treasure of industrial history, Slater's mill in Pawtucket, Rhode Island, is commonly considered the first successful factory in the nation.

Above; Textile workers holding shuttles, around 1870. Young women from the New England countryside became the first American factory workers.

Singer sewing machine
advertisement, around 1860

**Sewing Machine, patented
by Elias Howe, 1846 (Above)**

**Sewing Machine, patented
by Isaac Singer, 1851 (Right)**

Mechanizing the handcraft of
sewing was a technical challenge
that thwarted inventors for years.
Elias Howe is credited by many with
developing the first practical sewing
machine in 1846, but initially it was
ignored by the public.

Isaac Singer patented some
improvements to the sewing machine,
but his big contribution was marketing.
Through staged competitions and the
use of installment credit plans, Singer
largely created consumer demand for
sewing machines.

Fleming's Original Penicillium Mold, 1928

In September 1928, British bacteriologist Alexander Fleming found something unusual growing in his laboratory. Mold had contaminated a plate of staphylococci, disease-causing bacteria. Where the mold had spread, the bacteria had disappeared.

Further research revealed that the mold, *Penicillium notatum*, produced a substance harmful to microorganisms but relatively nontoxic to animals and humans. During World War II, British and American scientists expanded on Fleming's discovery to develop the powerful antibiotic penicillin.

Penicillin
THE NEW LIFE-SAVING DRUG
Saves Soldiers' Lives!

Men who might have died will live...if you

Give this job Everything You've got!

World War II poster (*National Archives and Records Administration*)

SCIENTIFIC INSIGHTS

I n the quest to unlock the secrets of the physical world, science has revealed fundamental truths, devised solutions to age-old problems, and
posed challenging new questions. These treasures represent some of the key
discoveries and developments that have shaped the history of science
in American life. While they are products of careful observation
and experimentation, they often have had unexpected impacts far
beyond the laboratory.

Salk Polio Vaccine and Syringe, 1954–1955

J onas Salk used this syringe and these vials
of polio vaccine to immunize patients during the vaccine's clinical trial in 1954–1955.

Poliomyelitis, or infantile paralysis, was
the most dreaded disease in the U.S. for
much of the 20th century. Salk's vaccine used
inactivated, or "killed," poliovirus to trigger
an immune response against the disease.
On April 12, 1955, officials announced the
vaccine's success and launched a nationwide
immunization campaign. Within a generation,
new cases of polio nearly disappeared.

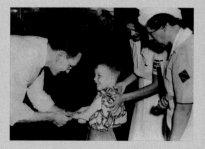

Administering the first shot of polio vaccine, 1954
(*March of Dimes*)

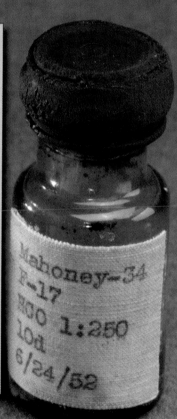

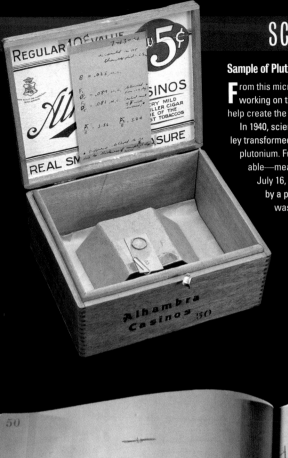

SCIENTIFIC INSIGHTS

Sample of Plutonium-239, 1941

From this microscopic sample of plutonium, scientists working on the Manhattan Project gained knowledge to help create the atomic bomb.

In 1940, scientists at the University of California at Berkeley transformed uranium into a new radioactive element, plutonium. Further testing proved plutonium was fissionable—meaning it could produce nuclear energy. On July 16, 1945, the world's first nuclear bomb, fueled by a plutonium core about the size of a baseball, was detonated near Alamogordo, New Mexico.

Nuclear explosion at Trinity test site, New Mexico, July 16, 1945 (*Los Alamos National Laboratory*)

Recombinant DNA Research Notebook, 1973

In this notebook, Stanford University professor Stanley Cohen described groundbreaking experiments that produced the first genetically engineered organisms.

Together with Herbert Boyer at the University of California at San Francisco, Cohen devised a method for transferring pieces of DNA from one bacterium to another in order to replicate, or clone, particular genes. The discovery sparked excitement over the medical and commercial potential of genetic recombination as well as fears about the ethics and safety of "tinkering" with DNA.

Spencer Microscope, around 1849–1859

Until Charles A. Spencer began making microscopes in Canastota, New York, in 1838, the only high-quality scientific instruments available in the U.S. were imported from Europe.

Spencer gained fame among American scientists for his fine objective lenses, which provided stronger magnification and sharper resolution than many European models. This brass monocular microscope, equipped with a mirror to reflect light through the slide, could be used with either a compound or a simple lens.

Time Magazine, April 18, 1977

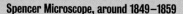

Röntgen X-ray of Albert von Kölliker's hand, made January 23, 1896

Röntgen X-ray Tube, around 1895

German physicist Wilhelm Conrad Röntgen, the discoverer of X-rays, used this vacuum tube in his early experiments. By applying electric current to the tube, he produced a mysterious type of radiation that could penetrate objects and form images on the other side.

Röntgen's discovery created an immediate international sensation, and physicians quickly adopted the X-ray for medical diagnosis and treatment. "Bone portraits" were also produced as novelties before the risks of radiation exposure were fully recognized.

AMERICAN BIOGRAPHY

Through its collections, the National Museum of American History preserves the stories of individuals who made history. Drawn from the worlds of politics, business, science, sports, arts, and entertainment, these objects represent people whose experiences and achievements earned them a place in the national spotlight. Examined individually, the lives presented here reflect the circumstances of their times and provide a personal perspective on the past. Together, they comprise a fascinating and multifaceted portrait of American achievement.

Jacqueline Kennedy's Gown, 1961

Made of silk chiffon and peau d'ange, this gown with matching cape was worn by Jacqueline Kennedy to her husband John F. Kennedy's presidential inaugural ball. The first lady worked with Ethel Frankau of Bergdorf-Goodman to design the gown.

A fashion trendsetter and cultural icon, "Jackie" brought a sense of youthful glamour and sophistication to life in the White House. After President Kennedy's assassination in 1963, the dignity and courage she displayed in mourning for her husband set a calming example for a bereaved nation.

Opposite: Jacqueline Kennedy (1929–1994)
Portrait by Richard Avedon (detail), 1961

Richard Avedon (1923–2004)

One of the 20th century's most influential photographers, Richard Avedon created striking portraits of authors, civic leaders, performers, and cultural icons from the 1950s until his death in 2004.

Avedon, the son of Russian-Jewish immigrants, learned the mechanics of photography in the U.S. Merchant Marine while taking thousands of identification photographs. In 1945 *Harper's Bazaar* hired Avedon as a staff photographer. His distinctive fashion and advertising photography captivated audiences, but his portraits with stark white backgrounds are among his most memorable works.

Self-portrait by Richard Avedon, 1978
(*National Portrait Gallery, Smithsonian Institution*)

Malcolm X (1925–1965)

A militant and charismatic proponent of black self-reliance, Malcolm X urged African Americans to unite against white oppression and secure their rights "by any means necessary."

In prison for burglary in the late 1940s, Malcolm X joined the separatist Nation of Islam. He later rose to international fame as a leading minister or orator. In 1964, he made the pilgrimage to Mecca where he experienced religious brotherhood that transcended race. In 1965, shortly after he had broken away from the Nation of Islam, Malcolm X was assassinated.

Malcolm X, by Richard Avedon, 1963
Avedon used a slightly out-of-focus camera to capture the emotional energy of his subject.

Marian Anderson (1897–1993)

The first African American to perform at the Met and among the greatest opera singers of her time, Anderson spent her entire career battling and breaking racial barriers. In one of her best-known performances, she sang on the steps of the Lincoln Memorial in 1939 after the Daughters of the American Revolution banned her from performing at Constitution Hall in Washington, D.C.

Marian Anderson, by Richard Avedon, 1955
Avedon photographed the famed contralto at the time of her debut at the Metropolitan Opera House in New York.

From a controversial collection titled *Nothing Personal*, Avedon's portrait of Dwight D. Eisenhower depicted the aged ex-president without his famous smile.

Dwight D. Eisenhower (1890–1969)

Having demonstrated his leadership as Supreme Commander of the Allied Forces during World War II, Eisenhower was elected U.S. president in 1952. With his amiable nature — immortalized by the campaign slogan, "I like Ike" — he projected a sense of optimism in a time of great challenges.

Eisenhower presided over a generally prosperous yet turbulent period in American history. He dealt with volatile issues, from escalating Cold War tensions, the Korean War, and McCarthyism to labor unrest and school desegregation.

Dwight D. Eisenhower, by Richard Avedon, 1964

Billy Graham (b. 1918)

One of the 20th century's most famous Christian evangelists, Billy Graham has inspired millions of Americans with his charismatic style and wide-reaching crusades.

The son of a prosperous dairy farmer, Graham began preaching in 1938. His national standing grew through tent revivals, radio, and later television broadcasts. He has served as spiritual advisor to many U.S. presidents, from Dwight Eisenhower to George W. Bush. Largely apolitical, Graham promotes the evangelical message of salvation through faith rather than good works alone.

Billy Graham, by Richard Avedon, 1964

Benjamin Franklin (1706–1790)

A celebrated writer, inventor, scientist, and advocate for U.S. independence, Benjamin Franklin rose from humble beginnings to become one of the most famous Americans of the 18th century.

The tenth child of a Boston candle maker, Franklin left home at age 17 to seek his fortune in Philadelphia. He established a successful printing business, became a civic leader, and invented practical devices including the lightning rod, the "Franklin" stove, and bifocals. Through advice and example, Franklin helped define the American ideal of self-improvement through virtue and hard work.

Background: Portrait by Joseph Siffred Duplessis, ca. 1785 (*National Portrait Gallery, Smithsonian Institution*)

Franklin Press, around 1720

According to tradition, Benjamin Franklin used this English common press while working as a journeyman in a London printing office in 1726. Franklin first learned the printing trade in Boston, as an apprentice to his brother James. He later opened his own print shop in Philadelphia, and in 1732 he began publishing his famous *Poor Richard's Almanack*.

Benjamin Franklin's Walking Stick, 1783

A French admirer presented this gold-capped walking stick to Benjamin Franklin while he was serving as ambassador to France. Franklin later bequeathed the cane to his friend and fellow revolutionary George Washington, declaring, "If it were a Sceptre, he has merited it, and would become it."

Maria Mitchell's Telescope

Pioneering astronomer Maria Mitchell (1818–1889) used this telescope, built by Henry Fitz in 1863, while she was a professor at Vassar College from 1865 to 1888. In this photograph, taken at the Vassar observatory around 1877, Mitchell is seated beside the telescope; her student Mary Whitney stands to the right.

From a young age, Mitchell displayed a keen interest in astronomy and spent many nights observing the skies. She achieved international recognition in 1847 for discovering a comet, and became one of the first women formally accepted into the American scientific community. A strong advocate for women's higher education, Mitchell encouraged women to realize their intellectual potential.

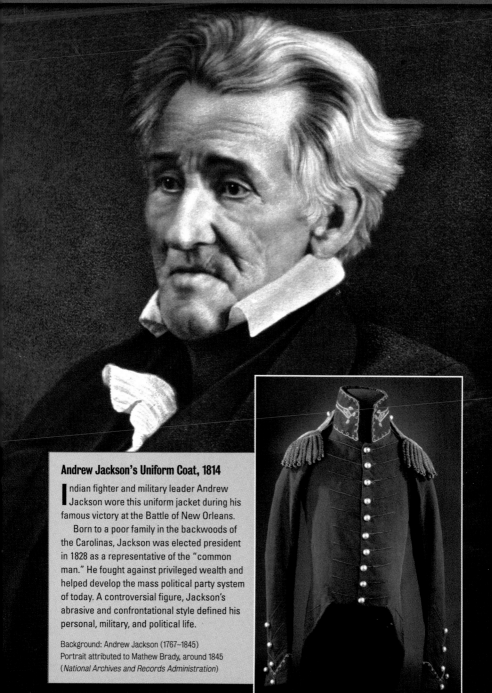

Andrew Jackson's Uniform Coat, 1814

Indian fighter and military leader Andrew Jackson wore this uniform jacket during his famous victory at the Battle of New Orleans.

Born to a poor family in the backwoods of the Carolinas, Jackson was elected president in 1828 as a representative of the "common man." He fought against privileged wealth and helped develop the mass political party system of today. A controversial figure, Jackson's abrasive and confrontational style defined his personal, military, and political life.

Background: Andrew Jackson (1767–1845)
Portrait attributed to Mathew Brady, around 1845
(*National Archives and Records Administration*)

Mary Todd Lincoln's Gown, 1861–1865

Worn by First Lady Mary Todd Lincoln, this purple velvet gown trimmed with white satin and French lace is believed to have been made by Elizabeth Keckley, a former slave who became Lincoln's dressmaker and confidante.

Mary Todd Lincoln (1818–1882)

As first lady, Mary Lincoln confronted prejudice, suspicion, and ridicule in her efforts to fit in to Washington society. Despite being well educated, the Kentucky native was belittled for her "frontier" roots. By demonstrating her good taste and skills as a hostess, she hoped to prove her loyalty and sophistication and advance her husband's political standing. Yet her extravagant spending on clothes, furnishings, and receptions only drew more criticism. Devastated by her husband's assassination in 1865, she struggled with depression and failing health for the rest of her life.

Elizabeth Keckley (1818?–1907)

Born into slavery, Elizabeth Keckley used her dressmaking skills to buy her freedom in 1855. She became a prominent figure in Washington's black community, organizing relief and educational programs for emancipated slaves. In 1868 she published her memoir, *Behind the Scenes, or, Thirty Years a Slave, and Four Years in the White House.* Mary Lincoln felt betrayed by Keckley's disclosure of private details about the Lincoln family, and the two friends never saw each other again.

(*The Lincoln Museum, Fort Wayne, IN, #3189*)

Susan B. Anthony's Shawl, around 1900

When Susan B. Anthony appeared in public to advocate for women's rights, she often wore this red silk shawl, which became her visual trademark.

Anthony's father, a Quaker abolitionist, encouraged his daughter's education and instilled in her a keen sense of social justice. First active in the temperance movement, she became focused on women's rights and led a nationwide campaign for a women's suffrage amendment. This goal was ultimately achieved in 1920, 14 years after Anthony's death, a testament to her famous motto: "Failure is impossible."

Susan B. Anthony (1820–1906)

Margaret Mead's Field Dress, 1920s

Worn by anthropologist Margaret Mead in Papua New Guinea, this cotton print dress has an adjustable fit to accommodate weight loss in the field.

Mead's extensive fieldwork in the South Pacific established her as an expert on cultural behavior. Believing anthropology could be a tool for positive social change, she became a celebrity, speaking out on issues such as women's rights, the nuclear arms race, and the "generation gap," a term she popularized.

Margaret Mead (1901–1978) with children of Manus Island, 1928 (Reo Fortune, courtesy of the Institute for Intercultural Studies, Inc., New York)

Patsy Cline's Outfit, around 1960

Made for country music star Patsy Cline by her mother, this Western-style outfit features record-shaped patches stitched with the titles of Cline's singles.

Cline began singing with gospel and country bands as a teenager in Virginia. With her 1957 breakout hit "Walkin' after Midnight," she became the first female country vocalist to cross over to the pop charts. In 1960, Cline achieved her childhood dream of joining the Grand Ole Opry in Nashville. Three years later, she died tragically in a plane crash.

Background: Patsy Cline (1932–1963)
(*AP/WideWorld Photos*)

Sandra Day O'Connor's Robe, 1981

The first female justice on the U.S. Supreme Court, Sandra Day O'Connor, wore this black judicial robe to her swearing-in ceremony on September 25, 1981.

Nominated by President Ronald Reagan, O'Connor developed her legal expertise as an attorney, state senator, and judge in Arizona. As a moderate conservative on the divided Rehnquist Court, she frequently cast deciding votes on controversial issues such as abortion, affirmative action, and the separation of church and state. She retired in 2005.

Right: Sandra Day O'Connor (b. 1930) at swearing-in ceremony, 1981 (*Office of the Curator, Supreme Court of the United States*)

Ed Roberts's Wheelchair, around 1978

Equipped with a sports-car seat, go-cart wheels, and a top speed of eight miles an hour, this wheelchair belonged to disability-rights pioneer Ed Roberts.

Roberts was paralyzed by polio in 1953, at age 14. In 1962 he enrolled at the University of California at Berkeley, where he led efforts to establish a program for disabled students. He later founded the Independent Living Movement, a worldwide campaign to secure civil rights, equal access, and self-sufficiency for people with disabilities.

Inset: Ed Roberts (1939–1995) at a disability rights protest, 1980s

Cesar Chavez's Union Jacket, around 1990

This jacket was worn by the famed labor activist Cesar Chavez.

As a teenager Chavez experienced the privations of migrant farm laborers in California. The founder and president of the United Farm Workers, he brought the plight of downtrodden agricultural workers to the national consciousness through strikes, marches, boycotts, and fasts. Chavez's success in community organizing and dedication to nonviolence earned him near mythic standing as a labor organizer and as an icon of Latino history.

Above: Cesar Chavez (1927–1993) leading a *peregrinación* (pilgrimage) from Delano to Sacramento, California, to popularize his grape boycott, March 17, 1966 (© George Ballis/Take Stock)

Ray Charles's Sunglasses, around 2002. These Ray-Ban sunglasses were Ray Charles's celebrity trademark.

Ray Charles's Tuxedo, 2002 "The Father of Soul Music" wore this sequined tuxedo during a 2002 concert in Rome.

Ray Charles (1930–2004)

Born into poverty and blinded by glaucoma at age seven, Ray Charles overcame great obstacles to gain world-wide acclaim as a singer, composer, and pianist. His emotive delivery and distinctive gravelly voice, together with his genius for crossing musical genres, produced many memorable hits, from rollicking soul tunes and country ballads to his celebrated rendition of "America the Beautiful."

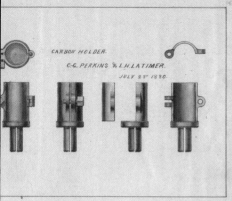

CARBON HOLDER.

C.G. PERKINS & L.H. LATIMER.

JULY 23ʳᵈ 1880.

Lewis Latimer Drawing, 1880

Electricity pioneer Lewis Latimer drew this component of an arc lamp, an early type of electric light, for the U.S. Electric Lighting Company in 1880.

The son of escaped slaves and a Civil War veteran at age 16, Latimer trained himself as a draftsman. His technical and artistic skills earned him jobs with Alexander Graham Bell and Thomas Edison, among others. An inventor in his own right, Latimer received numerous patents and was a renowned industry expert on incandescent lighting.

Lewis Latimer (1848–1928)
(*New York Public Library*)

Helen Keller's Watch, around 1880

Specially designed with pins around the case edge to mark the hours, this Swiss-made "touch watch" was one of Helen Keller's prized possessions.

As a baby, Keller contracted an illness that left her completely deaf and blind. After years of frustrated isolation, she met educator Annie Sullivan, who taught Keller to communicate by spelling words into her hand. Keller eventually learned to read, write, and speak, and attended Radcliffe College. Her inspiring story made her an international celebrity, and she became a prominent spokesperson for disability rights.

Helen Keller (1880–1968) reading Braille, 1907
(*Library of Congress*)

Babe Ruth Autographed Baseball, around 1930

The New York Yankees' legendary "Sultan of Swat" signed this baseball for a fan during a visit to Scranton, Pennsylvania.

A neglected and delinquent child, Ruth discovered his love for baseball while living at St. Mary's Industrial School for Boys in Baltimore. He began his major-league career as a star pitcher, but was reassigned to the outfield due to his powerful swing. With his record-setting home runs—60 in one season, 714 career total—and larger-than-life personality, Ruth thrilled fans and redefined the character of America's national pastime.

Left: Babe Ruth (1895–1948) (*Library of Congress*)

Louis Armstrong's Cornet, around 1913

Louis Armstrong received his first music lessons as a young inmate at the New Orleans Colored Waif's Home for Boys. After his release he continued to study music and reputedly received lessons on this cornet.

Armstrong first came to national prominence in 1920s Chicago. Through his remarkable sense of swing and his brilliant improvisations as a trumpeter and singer, he revolutionized jazz—transforming it from ensemble music into a soloist's art. Known for his humanitarianism, "Ambassador Satch" brought jazz to audiences around the globe.

Background: Louis Armstrong (1901–1971)

Muhammad Ali (b. 1942)
training for the "Rumble
in the Jungle," 1974
(*AP/WideWorld Photos*)

Muhammad Ali's Gloves, around 1975

Prizefighter Muhammad Ali, "The Greatest," wore these Everlast gloves while defending the second of his three world heavyweight championships.

An inspiring role model to many, the charismatic and outspoken Ali also generated controversy. During the Vietnam War, the champion was stripped of his title and banned from boxing after he refused to be drafted. His objection, based on his Muslim beliefs, was ultimately upheld by the Supreme Court. In a heroic comeback, he recaptured the championship in the "Rumble in the Jungle" against George Foreman in 1974.

PRESIDENT

John L. Lewis (1880–1969) announcing a truce in the coal strike of 1943

John L. Lewis's Union Badge, 1936

John Lewis, one of America's foremost labor leaders, wore this badge at the 1936 United Mine Workers of America (UMWA) convention.

Born in an Iowa coal mining camp, Lewis went to work in the mines at age 15. He rose quickly as a labor leader, becoming president of the UMWA in 1920, and later helped found the Congress of Industrial Organizations. Lewis led a successful struggle to organize industrial workers, improving wages, safety, and benefits.

INTERNATIONAL CONVENTION WASHINGTON, D.C.

19 36

U. M. W. OF AMERICA ORG 1890

Albert Einstein (1879–1955)
Portrait by Philippe Halsman, 1947
(*National Portrait Gallery, Smithsonian Institution*)

Albert Einstein's Pipe, around 1948

After doctors advised him to give up smoking, Albert Einstein continued to chew on this briar pipe out of habit and, perhaps, for inspiration.

Einstein, the Nobel Prize–winning physicist and creator of the theory of relativity, radically revised our concepts of space, time, and matter. After living and teaching in many countries, the German-born Einstein became a U.S. citizen in 1940. An outspoken pacifist, through his famous energy-mass equation, $E=mc^2$, ironically he laid the foundation for the development of the atomic bomb.

Marilyn Monroe's Gloves, around 1960

A seductive accessory fit for a sex symbol, these kidskin evening gloves were worn by actress Marilyn Monroe.

Norma Jean Baker, discovered working in a factory, became Marilyn Monroe when she signed her first movie contract in 1946. While her screen roles emphasized beauty over brains—most famously in *Gentlemen Prefer Blondes* (1953)—Monroe at times transcended the "dumb blonde" stereotype with gifted comedic and dramatic performances. As a superstar overshadowed by a tragic personal life, she remains one of Hollywood's most alluring icons.

Marilyn Monroe (1926–1962)
Portrait by Milton H. Greene, 1955
(© 2006 Joshua Greene, www.archiveimages.com)

Julia Child's Kitchen, 2001

In this fully equipped and highly personalized kitchen, celebrity chef Julia Child prepared meals for friends and family as well as for television audiences around the world.

Trained at the Cordon Bleu cooking school in Paris, Child brought the taste and techniques of traditional French cuisine into American homes. Her first series, *The French Chef*, premiered on Boston public television in 1962. Over her 40-year career, she produced numerous cookbooks and television cooking shows, including three filmed in the 1990s in her own kitchen in Cambridge, Massachusetts. In 2001, Child donated her famous kitchen to the Smithsonian.

Above: Julia Child (1912–2004) as "The French Chef" (*Schlesinger Library, Radcliffe Institute, Harvard University*)

Left: Handwritten recipe for *pain de mie*, or French sandwich bread, from Julia Child's kitchen, 2001

NATIONAL CHALLENGES

I n its role as a keeper of the nation's past, the National Museum of American History has documented many struggles, conflicts, and controversies that have challenged and shaped the nation. An unusual kind of museum treasure, these valuable pieces of history provide a broad and complex view of the American experience. By understanding the challenges of the past, Americans can draw important lessons and inspiration for confronting new challenges in the present and future.

Above right: Abraham Lincoln (1809–1865) Portrait by Alexander Gardner, February 1865 (*Library of Congress*)

Abraham Lincoln's Hat, 1865

P resident Lincoln wore this top hat to Ford's Theatre on April 14, 1865, the night he was assassinated by Confederate sympathizer John Wilkes Booth.

In his struggle to preserve a divided nation and extend the founding ideals of freedom and equality, Lincoln confronted the most critical and difficult challenges ever faced by an American president. Widely criticized during his presidency and blamed for a devastating civil war, after his death Lincoln became revered as a martyr and hero who saved the Union and abolished the evil of slavery.

Background: *Field Where General Reynolds Fell*, Gettysburg, July 1863, by Timothy O'Sullivan

In July 1776, the thirteen colonies declared independence from England and created a new nation, the United States of America. The American Revolution was inspired by revolutionary ideas—equality, liberty, and people's right to govern themselves—that would guide the future of American society and influence nations around the world. To this day, the struggle to uphold those founding ideals remains our fundamental national challenge.

George Washington's Candle Stand, 1796

By the light of this brass candelabrum, President Washington worked on his Farewell Address to the nation, which was published in September 1796.

After serving two terms as U.S. president, Washington opted not to seek a third—an example followed by all presidents but one, until term limits were officially imposed. In his Farewell Address, Washington urged Americans to uphold the Constitution and guard against divisive influences that could threaten national unity, including sectional self-interests, party politics, and alliances with foreign governments.

George Washington's Battle Sword, 1770s

General Washington carried this sword while commanding the Continental Army during the War of Independence. In his will, he instructed his heirs to use it only in "self-defense or in the defense of [the] country and its rights."

In leading his army, Washington regarded himself as a servant of the people, and deferred to the authority of the Continental Congress. He also refused pay for his military service. After the war ended, Washington surprised those who expected him to seize power, instead resigning his commission and returning to private life.

George Washington's Uniform, 1790s

The nation's first commander-in-chief wore this general officer's uniform during his presidency. (The coat, waist-coat, and breeches are original; the shirt and neckcloth are reproductions.)

George Washington's heroic military command during the American Revolution led to his unanimous election as the first U.S. president in 1789. In fulfilling his duties under the newly ratified Constitution, he demonstrated strong and effective leadership and established a precedent for all others to follow.

General Washington at Princeton
Painting by Charles Peale Polk, 1790

Thomas Jefferson's Desk, 1776

In June 1776, Thomas Jefferson drafted the Declaration of Independence on this mahogany writing box of his own design.

The Declaration asserted the colonists' right to revolt against English rule by invoking the principles of equality, liberty, and self-government. For Jefferson and his fellow founders, these rights applied only to people like themselves—free white men who owned property. But in proclaiming that "all men are created equal," the Declaration gave others a basis to claim those rights in the future.

Background: Engraving of the Declaration of Independence (National Archives and Records Administration)

776.

America.

Declaration of Independence
Painting by John Trumbull, 1817–1819
(*Architect of the Capitol*)

Census Jug, around 1790

Made in England for the American market, this creamware jug commemorates the first census of the United States taken in 1790.

The Constitution, adopted in 1787, mandated that the population of the states be counted every ten years to ensure proper representation in Congress. The first census, undertaken by U.S. marshals on horseback, recorded 3.9 million inhabitants in these categories: heads of families, free white males 16 years of age and older, free white males younger than 16, free white females, all other free persons (by sex and color), and slaves.

Gunboat *Philadelphia*, 1776

A naval relic from the War of Independence, this wooden warship was sunk by a British cannonball during the Battle of Valcour Island on October 11, 1776.

The *Philadelphia* was part of a small American fleet on Lake Champlain, where the British planned to invade the colonies from the north. Under the command of Benedict Arnold, the gunboats waged a valiant fight against the superior British navy. Although the Americans lost the battle, they succeeded in delaying the British advance, which proved to be a critical turning point in the war.

A VIEW of the BOM

The Star-Spangled Banner

O n September 14, 1814, this 30-foot-high flag was raised over Baltimore's Fort McHenry to signal a crucial American victory in the War of 1812. The sight inspired Francis Scott Key, who had witnessed the battle from a ship in the harbor, to write a poem that eventually became America's national anthem.

Less than thirty years after winning independence, the U.S. again went to war with Britain – this time to assert its rights as a sovereign nation and attempt an expansionist takeover of Canada. Though it ended in stalemate, the War of 1812—popularly called the Second War of Independence—generated a new spirit of nationalism among the American people.

A View of the Bombardment of Fort McHenry
Print by J. Bower, 1816

One of the greatest challenges to ever face the United States was the institution of slavery. Violent and inhumane, slavery affected millions of African Americans and created conflict between the North and the South.

While slavery existed as early as 1619 in colonial America, dependence on slave labor in the South did not become widespread until the late 1700s. Under the U.S. Constitution, slaves were defined as property, not citizens, and were given no rights. Slavery in the United States was not banned until the passage of the 13th Amendment in 1865.

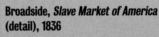

$150 REWARD

RANAWAY from the subscriber, on the night of the 2d instant, a negro man, who calls himself *Henry May*, about 22 years old, 5 feet 6 or 8 inches high, ordinary color, rather chunky built, bushy head, and has it divided mostly on one side, and keeps it very nicely combed; has been raised in the house, and is a first rate dining-room servant, and was in a tavern in Louisville for 18 months. I expect he is now in Louisville trying to make his escape to a free state, (in all probability to Cincinnati, Ohio.) Perhaps he may try to get employment on a steamboat. He is a good cook, and is handy in any capacity as a house servant. Had on when he left, a dark cassinett coatee, and dark striped cassinett pantaloons, new---he had other clothing. I will give $50 reward if taken in Louisvill; 100 dollars if taken one hundred miles from Louisville in this State, and 150 dollars if taken out of this State, and delivered to me, or secured in any jail so that I can get him again. WILLIAM BURKE.

Bardstown, Ky., September 3d, 1838.

Runaway Slave Ad

During the 1840s, an abolitionist network known as the Underground Railroad helped many slaves escape to freedom. In response to Southern pressure, Congress passed the Fugitive Slave Law of 1850, which made it illegal to harbor escaped slaves and obligated citizens in free states to assist slaveholders with the recapture of runaways. While some in the North resented the law, many others believed runaway slaves should be returned.

Broadside, *Slave Market of America* (detail), 1836

The importation of slaves to the United States was banned in 1808, but ownership of slaves remained legal in many states North and South. The interstate slave trade was big business and the source of wealth for some of the nation's richest citizens. As agricultural patterns changed, many slaves in the North and upper South were sold and marched to the Deep South. An estimated 600,000 slave families were broken up by sale in the years 1820–1860.

Jar Made by "Dave," 1862

Inscribed by its maker, a slave potter, the poem on this jar reads, "I made this jar all of cross / If you don't repent, you will be lost."

A few slaves gained a measure of independence. David Drake, or "Dave," as he signed his pieces, worked at the Lewis Miles plantation in Edgefield, South Carolina. In a state that outlawed literacy among slaves, Dave defiantly proclaimed his ability to read and write by signing his name and sometimes inscribing poetry on the stoneware vessels he made.

Cotton Gin Model, around 1796

In 1794, Eli Whitney patented a new kind of cotton gin. His invention, using rotating brushes and teeth to remove the seeds from cotton, was quickly copied and improved by others.

Southern plantation owners depended on slaves for labor-intensive crops such as rice, sugar, tobacco, and especially cotton. As the market demand for cotton increased in the early 1800s, the Southern cotton industry expanded dramatically, as did the system of slave labor it relied upon.

Slave Tag, 1833

In the early 19th century, the city of Charleston, South Carolina, required slaves to wear identifying tags like this one, marked "Servant."

Considered property, slaves did not always work for their owners but were sometimes rented out. In a few areas, hired slaves were forced to wear badges lest they be confused with free blacks.

Antislavery Medallion, about 1787

English ceramic manufacturer Josiah Wedgwood was also an active abolitionist. In 1787 he designed this jasperware cameo medallion, featuring a kneeling slave and the motto "Am I not a man and a brother?"

Distributed in both England and the United States, the medallions helped popularize the abolitionist cause. Benjamin Franklin, president of the first American antislavery society, wrote to Wedgwood: "I am persuaded [the medallion] may have an Effect equal to that of the best written Pamphlet in procuring favour to those oppressed people."

Pike from John Brown's Raid, 1859

On October 16, 1859, militant abolitionist John Brown and his small group of followers, armed with pikes and guns, seized the federal arsenal at Harpers Ferry, Virginia. Brown hoped to raise an army of freed slaves and invade the South. The plan failed, and Brown was executed for treason.

For some, mainly in the North, John Brown was a martyr to the just cause of ending slavery. Others, mainly in the South, viewed him as a terrorist.

Background: John Brown, 1859 (*Library of Congress*)

Below: "Harper's Ferry Insurrection," from *Frank Leslie's Illustrated Newspaper*, November 5, 1859 (*Library of Congress*)

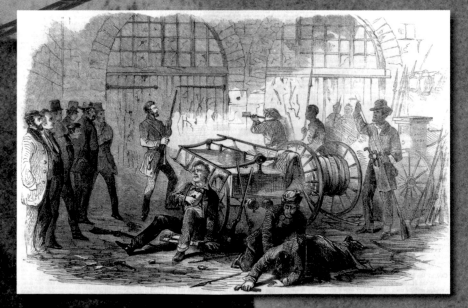

WESTERN EXPANSION

During the 1800s, the United States expanded westward, across the Mississippi and eventually to the Pacific Ocean. These western lands, already inhabited for centuries, were purchased, won, and seized outright from Indian tribes and other nations. As migrants came in search of wealth and better opportunities, they encountered and often clashed with Mexicans and Indians seeking to defend their homelands and traditional ways of life. These artifacts evoke the challenges that western expansion presented to those on both sides of the frontier.

Lewis and Clark Compass, around 1804

From 1804 to 1806, Meriwether Lewis and William Clark led an expedition through the Louisiana Purchase, the western territory acquired from France in 1803. This pocket compass was purchased by Lewis for the expedition.

Lewis and Clark's mission, assigned by President Jefferson, was to assess the land's resources, make diplomatic contact with Indians, and search for the fabled Northwest Passage, a water route to the Pacific Ocean. The 33-member party included two French-Canadian fur traders and a young Shoshone woman, Sacagawea, who served as guides and interpreters.

Cheyenne picture. Warrior killing a soldier. 176622

"Warrior Killing a Soldier," 1894

Drawn by a Cheyenne military prisoner, this picture shows a mounted Indian warrior charging toward a line of U.S. troops.

After the Civil War, the U.S. government launched a campaign of invasion, relocation, and extermination against the tribes of the Great Plains to secure western lands for white settlement. By 1890, soldiers had suppressed all armed opposition and forced the last resisters onto reservations. Indian artists, working on paper instead of traditional buffalo hides, recorded the bloody battles along with memories of a lost way of life.

Cherokee Pistol, 1843

The inscriptions on this pistol, in English and Cherokee, identify it as the work of Salola, a blacksmith for the Oconaluftee Cherokee of western North Carolina.

In 1838, 16,000 Cherokee were forced west to Oklahoma on the brutal "Trail of Tears" after refusing to relinquish lands in Georgia, where gold was discovered in 1829. Salola's people were among a small number of Cherokee, known today as the Eastern Band, who avoided removal and secured the right to remain in their homeland.

Map of Lewis and Clark expedition route, from drawing by William Clark (*Library of Congress*)

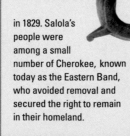

$10 Gold Coin, 1854

Made of California gold, this rare coin was one of the first produced at the U.S. Mint branch in San Francisco.

California gold initially had to be shipped to the U.S. Mint in Philadelphia, an expensive, slow, and risky undertaking. Meanwhile, private mints made coins that could be used in local markets. With the opening of the San Francisco Mint in 1854, gold could be converted quickly and efficiently into U.S. legal tender.

The mintmark, "S," is stamped on the reverse.

Below: The Roe family, Custer County, Nebraska
Photograph by Solomon D. Butcher, 1889
(*Nebraska State Historical Society*)

John Deere Plow, 1838

This steel plow, missing its original wooden handles, is the oldest John Deere plow known to exist. Its sharp steel share cut through the tough, root-filled sod of the Midwest, while its smooth, "self-scouring" moldboard prevented the sticky soil from clogging the plow.

Deere, an Illinois blacksmith, invented his plow in 1837; by 1850, he was producing 1,000 a year. Farmers using plows and other equipment transformed the Midwestern prairie into fertile farmland.

Gold from Sutter's Mill, 1848

On January 24, 1848, James Marshall found this tiny piece of yellow metal in the tailrace of John Sutter's sawmill in Coloma, California. When he hammered the nugget to test its malleability, it proved to be pure gold.

News of Marshall's discovery triggered one of the largest gold rushes in history. Drawing fortune-seekers from across the country and around the world, the gold rush hastened California's admission to statehood in 1850 and accelerated the cultural, environmental, and economic transformation of the American West.

Below: Gold miners in California, around 1850

Custer's Coat, 1870s

One of the West's most colorful and controversial figures, George Armstrong Custer wore this buckskin coat while leading the Seventh U.S. Cavalry on the Great Plains.

On an expedition in 1874, Custer confirmed the presence of gold in the Black Hills, a sacred hunting ground on the Lakota Indian reservation. A war over the territory ensued, with Custer leading the charge. On June 25, 1876, Custer's forces were annihilated at the Battle of Little Bighorn. But the Lakota victory was short-lived; in 1877, the tribe surrendered the Black Hills to the U.S. government.

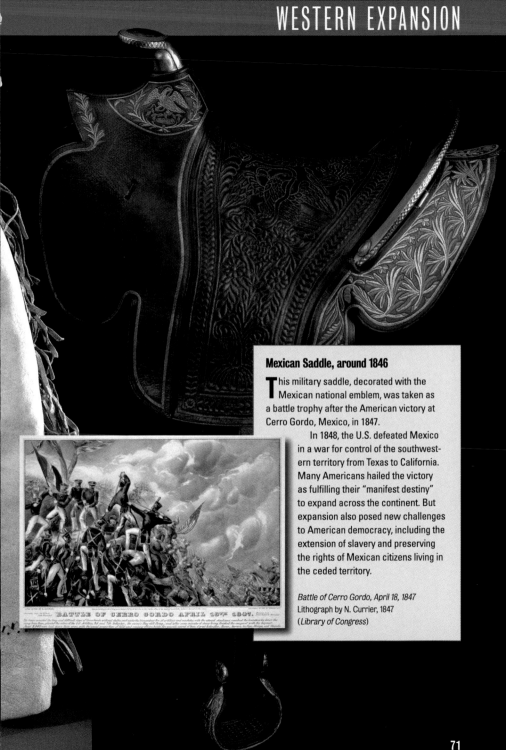

Mexican Saddle, around 1846

This military saddle, decorated with the Mexican national emblem, was taken as a battle trophy after the American victory at Cerro Gordo, Mexico, in 1847.

In 1848, the U.S. defeated Mexico in a war for control of the southwestern territory from Texas to California. Many Americans hailed the victory as fulfilling their "manifest destiny" to expand across the continent. But expansion also posed new challenges to American democracy, including the extension of slavery and preserving the rights of Mexican citizens living in the ceded territory.

Battle of Cerro Gordo, April 18, 1847
Lithograph by N. Currier, 1847
(*Library of Congress*)

THE CIVIL WAR

In April 1861, a decade of rising sectional tension over the expansion of slavery and the balance of power between slave and free states erupted into a full-scale civil war when Confederate forces attacked Fort Sumter, South Carolina.

The ensuing four years tested the United States in ways never experienced before or since. The deadliest of all American wars, the Civil War cost more than half a million lives and left 400,000 wounded. In preserving the Union and ending slavery, the war expanded the meaning of freedom and equality.

Below: U.S. National 34-Star Flag, 1861
Right: Confederate Battle Flag, 1861

Lincoln's Henry Rifle, around 1862

The New Haven Arms Company presented this engraved, gold-mounted Henry rifle to President Lincoln in hopes that he would endorse the innovative firearm for use by the Union army.

Designed by B. Tyler Henry, the .44-caliber lever-action repeating rifle fired up to seven times faster than single-shot muskets. Despite its technological advantages, it was deemed too heavy and damage-prone for regular battlefield use. After the Civil War, the Henry rifle was redesigned to create the famous 1866 Winchester rifle.

Right: Detail of engraving on rifle

President Lincoln on Battle-Field of Antietam
Photo by Alexander Gardner, October 1862

Gardner's Photographic Sketch Book of the War, 1866

The first published collection of Civil War photographs, this two-volume set features the work of Alexander Gardner and ten other photographers who traveled to camps, forts, and battlefields to document the four-year conflict.

In the 1860s, photo-illustrated books were expensive and painstaking to produce. Each volume of Gardner's *Sketch Book* contains 50 original albumen prints, mounted on boards and bound together with the accompanying text. Because of low public demand, only about 200 sets were printed, making this a rare treasure of American photographic history.

Ruins of Arsenal, Richmond, Virginia
Photo by Alexander Gardner, April 1863

Spotsylvania Stump, 1864

A mute testimony to the horrors of war, this shattered, bullet-riddled stump is all that remains of a large oak tree caught in the crossfire during one of the most ferocious battles of the Civil War.

On May 12, 1864, Union forces launched a frontal assault on the entrenched Confederate defenses around Spotsylvania Court House, Virginia. Twenty hours of intense hand-to-hand combat ensued, leaving thousands dead or wounded. The site of the worst fighting, near where this tree fell, became known as the Bloody Angle.

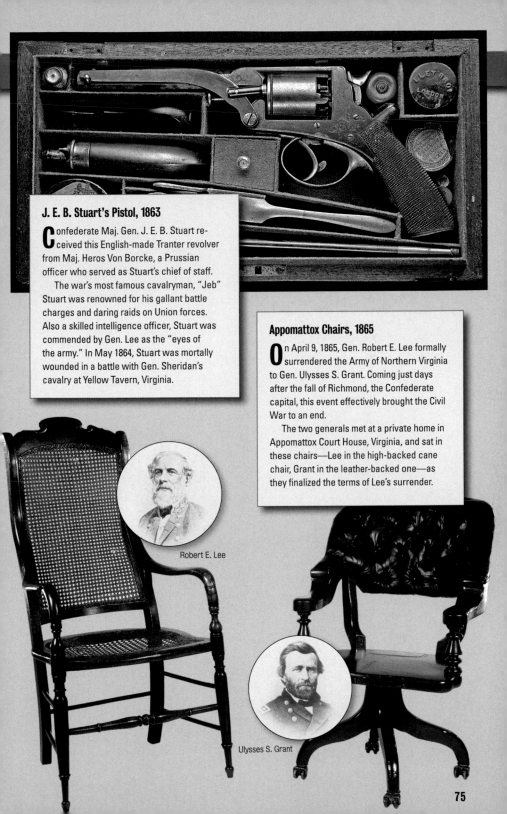

J. E. B. Stuart's Pistol, 1863

Confederate Maj. Gen. J. E. B. Stuart received this English-made Tranter revolver from Maj. Heros Von Borcke, a Prussian officer who served as Stuart's chief of staff.

The war's most famous cavalryman, "Jeb" Stuart was renowned for his gallant battle charges and daring raids on Union forces. Also a skilled intelligence officer, Stuart was commended by Gen. Lee as the "eyes of the army." In May 1864, Stuart was mortally wounded in a battle with Gen. Sheridan's cavalry at Yellow Tavern, Virginia.

Appomattox Chairs, 1865

On April 9, 1865, Gen. Robert E. Lee formally surrendered the Army of Northern Virginia to Gen. Ulysses S. Grant. Coming just days after the fall of Richmond, the Confederate capital, this event effectively brought the Civil War to an end.

The two generals met at a private home in Appomattox Court House, Virginia, and sat in these chairs—Lee in the high-backed cane chair, Grant in the leather-backed one—as they finalized the terms of Lee's surrender.

Robert E. Lee

Ulysses S. Grant

WOMEN'S SUFFRAGE

or more than a century, women in the United States struggled to obtain the right to vote. As they sought to claim their rights as citizens, they confronted deeply entrenched prejudices against women's participation in political life. In 1920, the suffrage movement finally achieved victory with the ratification of the 19th Amendment. Having won the vote, many women's rights activists continued to work toward a broader definition of social and political equality.

MR. PRESIDENT
HOW LONG
MUST
WOMEN WAIT
FOR LIBERTY

MR. PRESIDENT
WHAT
WILL YOU DO
FOR
WOMAN SUFFRAGE

Suffrage Sash, around 1910

or the suffragist who wore this yellow sash in the early 1900s, the color of the silk was as meaningful as the "Votes for Women" slogan printed on it.

After Kansas suffragists adopted the state symbol of the sunflower for a campaign in 1867, yellow became the symbolic color of the national women's suffrage movement. Supporters were urged to "show your colors" by wearing yellow ribbons, buttons, and sashes.

Above: Suffragists picketing the White House, 1917

VOTES FOR WOMEN

Amelia Walker's "Jailed for Freedom" Pin, 1917

Silver pins, representing a cell door with a heart-shaped padlock, were given by the National Woman's Party to members who had been "jailed for freedom."

In 1917, militant suffragists staged a months-long vigil outside the White House. Tolerated at first, the picketers drew increasing criticism after the U.S. entered World War I. Ninety women were arrested for "obstructing traffic" and sent to prison, where they suffered mistreatment and waged hunger strikes. The resulting publicity helped put pressure on Congress to consider a suffrage amendment.

Declaration of Sentiments Table, 1848

On this parlor table, Elizabeth Cady Stanton drafted the Declaration of Sentiments, a radical demand for equality that launched the first women's rights convention in Seneca Falls, New York.

Modeled after the Declaration of Independence, Stanton's document proclaimed that "all men and women are created equal" and resolved that women would take action to claim the rights of citizenship denied to them by men. The Declaration of Sentiments was adopted officially at the Seneca Falls Convention in July 1848 and signed by 68 women and 32 men.

Above: Announcement from *Seneca County Courier*, 1848 (*Library of Congress*)

Below: ERA supporters marching down Pennsylvania Avenue, Washington, D.C., 1978

ERA Charm Bracelet, 1972

In 1972, Congress passed the Equal Rights Amendment (ERA), which would guarantee men and women equal rights under state and federal law, and sent it to the states for ratification. This bracelet, representing 11 of the 35 states that ratified the ERA, was worn by Alice Paul, who drafted the original amendment in 1923.

From 1972 to 1982, supporters campaigned to get the required 38 states to ratify the amendment.

But the effort was opposed and ultimately defeated by those who feared the ERA's moral and legal impact on American society.

Background: Anti-ERA activist Phyllis Schlafly with demonstrators inside the Illinois state capitol, 1978 (© Bettmann/CORBIS)

Perhaps no two events shaped 20th-century America more profoundly
than the Great Depression and World War II. In this brief period, from
1929 to 1945, a generation of Americans faced terrible fears and achieved
great triumphs. Their experiences would leave a lasting impact on the
nation's history and memory.

Emergency Money, 1933

When the nation's banks closed during the Depression, Leiter's Pharmacy in Pismo Beach, California, issued this clamshell as change.

The 1929 stock market crash triggered banking panics, as people rushed to withdraw their savings before they were lost. In March 1933, President Roosevelt ordered a four-day bank holiday to prevent further runs. To compensate for the currency shortage, communities created emergency money, or scrip. This clamshell was signed as it changed hands and redeemed when cash became available again.

"Fireside Chat" Microphone, 1930s

This National Broadcasting Company microphone was used by President Franklin D. Roosevelt to broadcast radio addresses known as "fireside chats."

Through these informal talks, delivered between 1933 and 1944, Roosevelt developed an intimate, reassuring rapport with the American people that helped build confidence in his leadership. In his first broadcast on March 12, 1933, Roosevelt explained his plan to deal with the banking crisis and asked for the public's support, concluding, "Together we cannot fail."

President Roosevelt delivering radio address

Migrant Mother by Dorothea Lange, 1936

During the Great Depression, government photographer Dorothea Lange took this picture at a migrant farm workers' camp near Nipomo, California. Lange's brief caption recorded her impressions of the family's plight: "Destitute pea pickers . . . a 32-year-old mother of seven children."

First published in a San Francisco newspaper, the poignant image became one of the most famous photographs of the Depression era, emblematic of the hardships suffered by poor migrant families. The "migrant mother," anonymous for many years, was later identified as Oklahoma native Florence Thompson.

We Can Do I

Poster, *We Can Do It!*, 1942

This work incentive poster was produced by artist J. Howard Miller for the Westinghouse Electric & Manufacturing Company. Though displayed only briefly in Westinghouse factories, the poster has become one of the most famous icons of World War II.

As women were encouraged to take wartime jobs in defense industries, Rosie the Riveter became a celebrated symbol of female patriotism. Yet when the war ended, most women were forced to relinquish their skilled jobs to returning veterans.

POST FEB. 15 TO FEB. 28

WAR PRODUCTION CO-ORDIN

D Day, by Robert Capa, 1944

Combat photographer Robert Capa captured this arresting image of American troops landing at Omaha Beach on June 6, 1944.

D day was the launching date for Operation Overlord, the Allied invasion of Nazi-occupied Western Europe. In one of the most complex operations in military history, U.S., British, and Canadian forces landed simultaneously on five separate beachheads in Normandy, France, and stormed through intense German artillery fire to establish a foothold. Three months later, Paris was liberated, and the Allied advance began to close in on Germany.

Japanese-American families boarding bus for Manzanar (*Library of Congress*)

Internment Camp Sign, around 1942–1945

This sign identified the barracks residence of Michibiku Ozamoto, a Japanese American interned at Manzanar, California, during World War II.

On February 19, 1942, President Roosevelt signed Executive Order 9066, authorizing the internment of people of Japanese descent in the interest of national security. Almost 120,000 men, women, and children, the majority of them U.S. citizens, were forced from their homes into detention camps. In 1988, Congress formally apologized for the internment and paid restitution to surviving internees.

CIVIL RIGHTS

In the mid-20th century, African Americans launched a renewed struggle to claim the civil rights that had long been denied to them. As they moved to end racial segregation, they called upon the nation

to live up to its ideals of freedom, equality, and democracy. Through peaceful yet determined action, they called attention to injustice, achieved major victories, and inspired other groups to mobilize for equal rights.

Greensboro Lunch Counter, 1960

On February 1, 1960, four African American college students protesting segregation entered a Woolworth's drugstore in Greensboro, North Carolina, sat down at this "whites-only" lunch counter, and politely asked to be served. When their request was denied, the students refused to leave.

For six months, students and supporters staged a sit-in protest and boycott of the store. In July 1960, the Woolworth's lunch counter was desegregated. A watershed event in the civil rights movement, the Greensboro sit-in led to similar protests across the South.

Above: Second day of the Greensboro sit-in, February 2, 1960. Two of the original protesters, Joseph A. McNeil and Franklin E. McCain, are joined by William Smith and Clarence Henderson. (*Greensboro News and Record*)

Opposite: Rev. Martin Luther King Jr. at the March on Washington for Jobs and Freedom, August 28, 1963 (*AP/WideWorld Photos*)

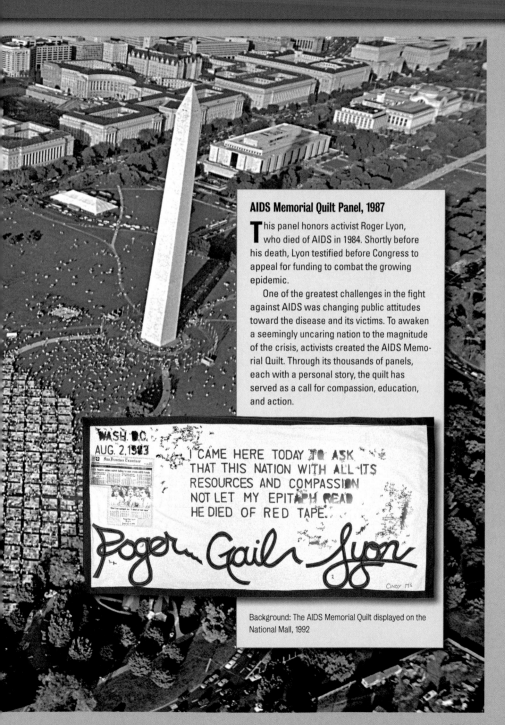

AIDS Memorial Quilt Panel, 1987

This panel honors activist Roger Lyon, who died of AIDS in 1984. Shortly before his death, Lyon testified before Congress to appeal for funding to combat the growing epidemic.

One of the greatest challenges in the fight against AIDS was changing public attitudes toward the disease and its victims. To awaken a seemingly uncaring nation to the magnitude of the crisis, activists created the AIDS Memorial Quilt. Through its thousands of panels, each with a personal story, the quilt has served as a call for compassion, education, and action.

WASH. D.C.
AUG. 2, 1983
San Francisco Examiner

I CAME HERE TODAY TO ASK
THAT THIS NATION WITH ALL ITS
RESOURCES AND COMPASSION
NOT LET MY EPITAPH READ
HE DIED OF RED TAPE.

Roger Gail Lyon

CINDY M's

Background: The AIDS Memorial Quilt displayed on the National Mall, 1992

Many of the National Museum of American History's treasures give insight into what it has meant to be an American. Culturally, Americans have defined themselves in many ways—through artistic expression, ethnic traditions, work and play, and home and community life. The Museum's collections reflect the diverse roots of American culture as well as common experiences shared across lines of race, ethnicity, and region.

Kermit the Frog, around 1970

The creation and alter ego of master puppeteer Jim Henson, Kermit the Frog is an American icon, recognized worldwide as the television star of *Sesame Street* and *The Muppet Show*.

For decades, Henson's adorably zany cast of Muppet characters has entertained children and adults alike with music, comedy, and life lessons. Kermit served as a crusader for tolerance through his hit song, "(It's Not Easy) Bein' Green."

Opposite: Jim Henson and the Muppets, 1988

AMERICAN HATS

A hat is much more than a practical way to keep one's head warm. As a symbol of identity, it also reveals much about the wearer's occupation, social class, cultural heritage, and personal style. Drawn from the Museum's vast collections, here is a fun sampling of hats worn by Americans at different times and places.

Background: Firefighter's Parade Helmet, 1883–1885, worn by Peter Zeluff, Assistant Chief Engineer **A** Construction Hard Hat, 2001, worn by iron worker Dennis Quinn during the World Trade Center recovery operation **B** Quaker Woman's Bonnet, 1850–1874 **C** Girl Scout's Beret, 1956–1968 **D** Lady's Ostrich-Feather Hat, 1910–1912 **E** Schoolboy's Cap, around 1910, Public School 49, New York City

A

B

C

Background Straw Hat, 1970s, worn by country-western comedienne Minnie Pearl **A** National Association for the Advancement of Colored People (NAACP) Cap, 1963, worn by civil rights activist Roy Wilkins during the March on Washington **B** Bride's Cap, 1929, worn by Eloise Tasher Moore, South Bend, Indiana **C** Woman's African-style Headwrap, 1972, worn by Fath Ruffins, Washington, D.C. **D** Union Cap, around 1937, worn by a member of the International Ladies' Garment Workers' Union (ILGWU) **E** Farmworker's Hat, 1940s, worn by Mexican guest worker (*bracero*) Savas Castro in California **F** Batting Helmet, around 1970, worn by Carl Yastrzemski of the Boston Red Sox

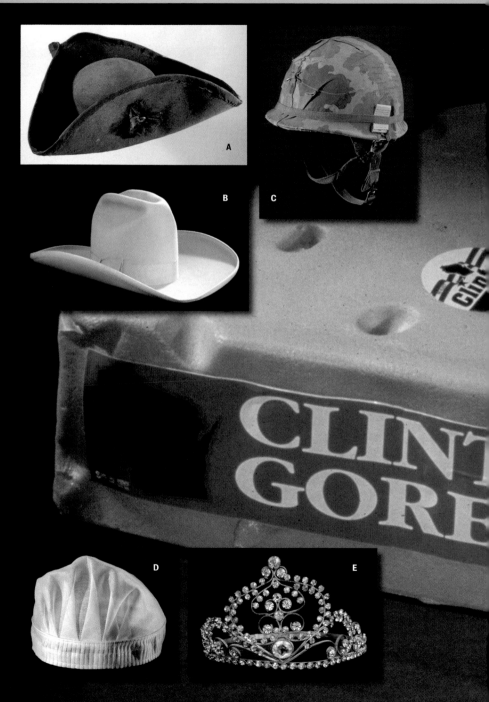

A

B

C

D

E

F

Background "Cheesehead" Hat, 1996, worn by Patricia Hawley, Wisconsin delegate to the Democratic National Convention **A** Tricorn Hat, 1776, worn by Colonel Jonathan Pettibone, 18th Regiment, Connecticut Militia **B** Cowboy Hat, around 1914, "Tom Mix" style, made by John B. Stetson Company **C** Camouflage Helmet, 1969, worn by U.S. soldier Terry Turner in Vietnam tracking the months remaining on his tour of duty **D** Nurse's Cap, 1945, worn by Elizabeth Brizindine, graduate of the Johns Hopkins Hospital School of Nursing **E** Miss America's Crown, 1951, worn by Yolande Betbeze **F** Carnival Mask (*carete de vejigante*), 1985, made by Miguel Caraballo of Ponce, Puerto Rico

Torah Mantle, 1785–1786

Made in Wenkheim, Germany, this silk Torah mantle was brought to San Francisco by Jewish immigrants during the California gold rush and presented to Congregation Emanu-El.

Founded in 1850, Emanu-El (Hebrew for "God is with us") was one of the first synagogues in San Francisco. It provided a spiritual and social community for German and Central European Jews who came to California in search of economic opportunities and political freedom.

The Constitution defines the United States as a nation committed to religious toleration. While Americans have often struggled to achieve that ideal, for centuries the promise of religious freedom has been a beacon to many immigrants, and today the U.S. remains one of the most religiously diverse countries in the world. These artifacts reflect some of the many expressions of faith that have shaped American history.

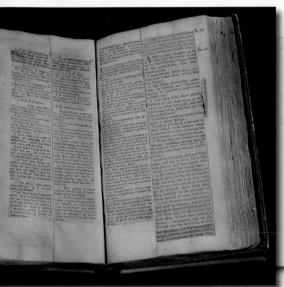

Jefferson Bible, around 1820

Near the end of his life, Thomas Jefferson clipped verses from the New Testament to create this work, *The Life and Morals of Jesus of Nazareth*. Reflecting Jefferson's deist beliefs, the book excludes references to miracles and focuses on Jesus' moral teachings.

Known as an advocate for a "wall of separation" between church and state, Jefferson believed spirituality was a private matter. But as president, he supported the symbolic role of religion in public life through such acts as attending church services in the Capitol.

Butsudan, around 1942–1945

Made in a Japanese-American internment camp in Poston, Arizona, during World War II, this Buddhist home shrine, or *butsudan*, provided a comforting connection to faith in a time of crisis.

Despite the freedom of worship guaranteed by the Constitution, many religious minorities have endured prejudice and persecution from mainstream Christian society. During World War II, Japanese-American Buddhists were pressured to abandon their religion and convert to Christianity to prove their loyalty to the United States.

Bradford Cup, 1634

This silver wine cup belonged to Pilgrim leader and Mayflower passenger William Bradford, who governed Plymouth Colony for 30 years. Made for Bradford in London, the cup bears his initials on one side.

The idea of America as a religious refuge originates with the Pilgrims, a group of English separatists who founded a colony at Plymouth, Massachusetts, in 1620. While the Pilgrims sought freedom to practice their own form of Protestantism, they did not tolerate other kinds of worship.

Pueblo Hide Painting, around 1700

Painted by an artist at Santo Domingo Pueblo in present-day New Mexico, this Catholic devotional image depicts Saint Anthony of Padua holding the infant Jesus.

In their efforts to convert the native population to Christianity, Spanish missionaries encouraged the Pueblo people to produce *santos*, images of saints, from local materials. In this painting, vegetable dyes were substituted for oil paints, and buffalo hide for canvas.

Bible Quilt, around 1885

The work of African-American quilter Harriet Powers, this renowned quilt depicts 11 stories from the Bible, including Adam and Eve in the Garden of Eden, the murder of Abel by Cain, the crucifixion of Jesus, and the Last Supper.

Powers was born a slave in Georgia in 1837. Like many enslaved African Americans, she infused the practice of Christianity with expressions of her cultural roots. Her Bible quilt features appliqué figures similar to those found on West African textiles.

Sun Stone from Mormon Temple, 1844

Inspired by a vision described by Joseph Smith, the founder of the Church of Jesus Christ of Latter-Day Saints (the Mormons), this celestial limestone carving was one of 30 that adorned a grand temple built at Nauvoo, Illinois, in the 1840s.

After Smith was murdered by an anti-Mormon mob in 1844, the congregation was driven out of Nauvoo and the temple destroyed. The Mormon community relocated to Utah, where it flourished in the isolation of the West.

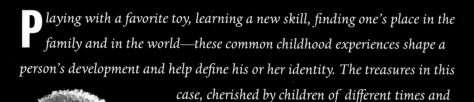

Playing with a favorite toy, learning a new skill, finding one's place in the family and in the world—these common childhood experiences shape a person's development and help define his or her identity. *The treasures in this case, cherished by children of different times and places, reflect different ideas about what it has meant to grow up American.*

Teddy Bear, around 1903

This is one of the earliest "Teddy" bears, created by a Brooklyn candy store owner who went on to form the Ideal Toy Company. Named after a president and inspired by an editorial cartoon, this beloved childhood companion has a unique political history.

In 1902, *Washington Post* cartoonist Clifford Berryman depicted President Theodore Roosevelt refusing to shoot a captured bear offered up as a hunting trophy. The bear became a regular figure in Berryman's cartoons, serving as a fuzzy, cuddly foil for the brawny president.

One of Clifford Berryman's "Teddy Bear" cartoons (*Library of Congress*)

Tin Toy, 1862

This jaunty horse-drawn carriage was presented to a little girl in Washington, D.C., during the Civil War.

When wound with a key, a clockwork mechanism inside the toy turns the back wheels and sends the carriage on its way. The toy's manufacturer, George W. Brown & Co., of Connecticut, was famous for producing a variety of windup tin toys during the mid-1800s.

Baby Bonnet, around 1920

Ng Shee Lee, a Chinese immigrant living in New York's Chinatown, made this silk bonnet for her American-born son, Peter.

Caps like this one are traditionally worn by Chinese boys after their first birthday. With its furry ears, the bonnet is meant to resemble the head of a dog, a disguise to protect the child from evil spirits.

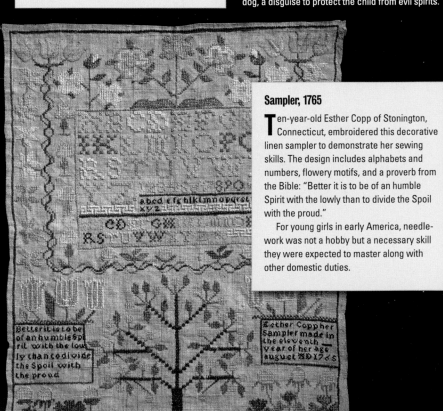

Sampler, 1765

Ten-year-old Esther Copp of Stonington, Connecticut, embroidered this decorative linen sampler to demonstrate her sewing skills. The design includes alphabets and numbers, flowery motifs, and a proverb from the Bible: "Better it is to be of an humble Spirit with the lowly than to divide the Spoil with the proud."

For young girls in early America, needlework was not a hobby but a necessary skill they were expected to master along with other domestic duties.

Baseball Card, 1952

This card, featuring New York Yankees outfielder Mickey Mantle, is from the first major set issued by the Topps Chewing Gum Company. Highly sought by collectors today, many of whom grew up watching Mantle play, it ranks as one of the most valuable cards from the post-World War II era.

First produced in the late 1800s as tobacco advertisements, baseball cards became popular collectibles for fans of all ages.

Barbie Doll, around 1960

In 1959, the Mattel toy company introduced the world to Barbie. Unlike most dolls at the time, Barbie was a grown-up—a "teenage fashion model" who could shop, date, drive, and fulfill other fantasies of young womanhood.

While often criticized for her unrealistic physical proportions and stereotypical attitude, Barbie has also evolved with the times. Since the 1980s she has taken on many new careers, from police officer to paleontologist, and even run for president.

Keds Sneakers, around 1957

These black canvas high-tops were worn by Jon Provost, the child actor who played "Timmy" on the television series *Lassie* (1957–1964). Like many young sneaker owners, Provost customized his Keds by doodling on the rubber soles with a marker.

Since their invention in the early 1900s, sneakers have been a mainstay of childhood fashion, valued for their comfortable fit and sturdy construction as well as their style.

Above: "Timmy and Lassie"

AMERICAN MUSIC

F rom folk songs to national anthems, jazz to rock and roll, popular music has expressed what it means to be American. Its cultural role expanded dramatically in the 20th century, as new technologies enabled music produced by local communities to be shared with and adapted for broader audiences. As a product of diverse traditions, talents, and techniques coming together in harmonious but also contentious ways, popular music is truly the soundtrack of the American experience.

The Sousa Band

Ma Rainey Record, 1924

A rare recording by classic blues singer Gertrude "Ma" Rainey, this 78-rpm disk features "Dream Blues" and "Lost Wandering Blues."

Billed as the Mother of the Blues, Rainey helped popularize the earthy, expressive music that emerged from the rural black South after the Civil War. The earliest blues recordings, made in the 1920s, were labeled "race records" and marketed to African-American audiences. Today the blues is recognized as the primary root of 20th-century American popular music, influencing jazz, rhythm and blues, country, and rock and roll.

John Philip Sousa's Baton, around 1892–1932

A merica's March King, John Philip Sousa, used this silver-tipped baton to conduct his world-famous band, which he led from 1892 to 1932.

A masterful composer of music to get people moving, Sousa also popularized classical music, first as leader of the U.S. Marine Band and then touring with his own Sousa Band. His stirring military marches, including "The Stars and Stripes Forever," expressed the nationalistic spirit of their times, but they have also gained an enduring appeal as part of the country's patriotic repertoire.

Dizzy Gillespie's Trumpet, 1972

Modern jazz virtuoso Dizzy Gillespie played this customized King "Silver Flair" trumpet from 1972 to 1985. He adopted the signature angled design in 1954, after someone accidentally bent his horn and he discovered he liked the sound that resulted.

In the 1940s, Gillespie helped develop an innovative style known as bebop, featuring intricate improvisations, complex harmonies, and rapid rhythms. The birth of modern jazz, bop was also a movement by African-American artists to reclaim jazz from the commercial mainstream and elevate it from dance music to a sophisticated art form.

Inset above: Dizzy Gillespie

Prince's Electric Guitar, 1989

Called the Yellow Cloud, this guitar was designed and played by Prince. The fingerboard
is decorated with the artist's personal icon, a
combination of male and female symbols.

Launched to superstardom by the 1984 album
Purple Rain, Prince has put his own singular
mark on American popular music as a performer,
songwriter, producer, and innovator. Blending influences that include funk, gospel, hip-hop, and
rock, his music has attracted broad appeal
and reflected his distinctive personality.

Prince in concert, 1986 (© *Neal Preston/CORBIS*)

Duke Ellington Score, around 1932–1942

In scoring music for his famous jazz orchestra, Duke Ellington wrote for individuals, not instruments. This "Mood Indigo" page features his trombone section: Joe "Tricky Sam" Nanton, Lawrence Brown, and Juan Tizol.

As a composer and bandleader, Ellington combined his players' individual sounds like an artist working from a palette. The distinctive results—from the hot jazz of Harlem's Cotton Club to classical-inspired suites and pop standards—earned Ellington and his band a legendary place in music history.

Left: Duke Ellington and orchestra

Tito Puente's Timbales, 1996

Bandleader and percussionist Tito Puente played these timbales during the closing ceremonies of the 1996 Olympics in Atlanta. Puente traditionally performed in front of the orchestra, a position that showcased his exuberant style.

A native of Spanish Harlem, Puente fused the Afro-Cuban rhythms of his Puerto Rican roots with jazz melodies to create sensational dance music. As one of the "Mambo Kings" of the 1950s, and later in collaboration with other jazz and salsa artists, he brought Latin sounds to the forefront of American popular culture.

Tito Puente in concert, 1991
(*AP/WideWorld Photos*)

Irving Berlin's Piano, 1940

Custom-made for songwriter Irving Berlin, this transposing upright piano can be played in any key using any notes. Berlin used it to write his 1942 hit "White Christmas," one of the top-selling songs of all time.

Berlin published nearly a thousand songs, from Tin Pan Alley sheet music to Broadway show tunes and the patriotic anthem "God Bless America." A Russian-Jewish immigrant, he adopted a "melting-pot" style, drawing from ragtime, blues, ballads, and other genres to produce a commercially popular and uniquely American sound.

"White Christmas," by Irving Berlin, 1942
"God Bless America," by Irving Berlin, 1938

All in the Family

Archie Bunker's Chair, 1970s

The popular and controversial sitcom *All in the Family* (CBS, 1971–1979) broke with convention and shattered taboos by depicting, in the words of creator Norman Lear, "real people dealing with real issues."

Social conflicts of the day played out in the Bunkers' living room as the bigoted Archie clashed with his liberal son-in-law and his wife, Edith, struggled to keep the peace. With sharp but affectionate humor, the show exposed the flaws and complexities of one American family.

Television expresses American identity in profound and influential ways. From news to cartoons, sitcoms to drama, programs have reflected the issues and values—if not always the realities—of the eras that produced them. As a source of information, ideas, and shared experiences, television has also shaped how we understand the present and remember the past.

The Lone Ranger's Mask, 1950s

Clayton Moore wore this black mask as the star of *The Lone Ranger* (ABC, 1949–1957), a Western about a Texas Ranger who disguises his identity to fight crime on the frontier.

Accompanied by his trusted Indian sidekick, Tonto, and packing a gun loaded with silver bullets, the Lone Ranger dispensed justice while respecting the laws of society. Week after week, he thrilled fans with his heroic adventures, virtuous conduct, and the stirring call to his white stallion: "Hi-yo Silver, away!"

The Lone Ranger

60 Minutes Stopwatch, 1970s–1990s

The most watched news program in American history, *60 Minutes* (CBS, 1968–) revolutionized television journalism with its pioneering newsmagazine format.

As conceived by producer Don Hewitt, the show includes a mix of breaking news, investigative reports, interviews, and commentary. The famous opening logo, a ticking stopwatch, also marks time between segments. This watch was used on the program until the late 1990s, when it was replaced by a computer graphic.

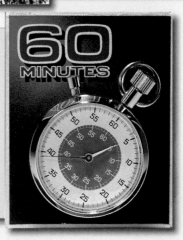

Seinfeld (Castle Rock Entertainment)

G1
4 cams 3A3, 3B3, 3C3, 3X

SEINFELD
"The Puffy Shirt"   Revision #1 (pink)
                                     Aug 30 1993

8:46:02
8:54:23

                    JERRY
I can't wear this puffy shirt on
tv. Look at it. It looks
ridiculous.

                    KRAMER
Jerry, you have to wear it. All
those stores are stocking it based
on the condition that you're going
to wear it on tv. The factory in
New Jersey is already making them.

                    JERRY
They're making these.

                    KRAMER
Jerry, this pirate trend she's
     going to be the look of
     . You'll be the first

          JERRY
     to be a pirate.

     KRAMER
listen-to-me!
     areer was floundering.

     lized her whole

     ERRY
     I put a sport jacket

Seinfeld's "Puffy Shirt," 1993

On a memorable episode of *Seinfeld* (NBC, 1989–1998), comedian Jerry Seinfeld unwittingly agrees to wear this frilly pirate shirt during an appearance on *The Today Show*.

The hit series, famously described as a show "about nothing," reveled in the absurd situations that emerged from the everyday lives of its four main characters: Jerry, George, Elaine, and Kramer. The "puffy shirt" episode, originally broadcast September 23, 1993, was written by *Seinfeld* co-creator Larry David.

Above: *Seinfeld* script for "The Puffy Shirt," by Larry David

Mister Rogers' Neighborhood
(Family Communications Inc.)

Mr. Rogers's Sweater, 1970s

This red knit cardigan was worn by Fred Rogers, creator and host of the children's program, *Mister Rogers' Neighborhood* (PBS, 1968–2001). For more than 30 years, Rogers began each episode by changing into a sweater and tennis shoes and singing, "Won't you be my neighbor?"

An ordained Presbyterian minister, Rogers dedicated his television career to promoting children's emotional and moral well-being. His show, with its friendly conversational style and trips to the "Neighborhood of Make-Believe," encouraged young viewers to feel loved, respected, and special.

Sex and the City (HBO)

Carrie Bradshaw's Laptop, 1998–2004

Manhattan newspaper columnist Carrie Bradshaw, played by Sarah Jessica Parker, used this laptop to record her observations on modern relationships in the risqué comedy series *Sex and the City* (HBO, 1998–2004).

Frank, witty, and often outrageous, the Emmy Award–winning cable show won millions of loyal fans with its depiction of four women friends and their romantic urban escapades. It also established cable TV as a competitive producer of original programming. *Sex and the City* set fashion trends, from Manolo Blahnik shoes to cosmopolitan cocktails, and provoked cultural debates about sex, relationships, and gender roles.

BOSTON

SEOUL 34 mi 54 km.

CONEY ISLAND 7033 MILES

SAN FRANCISCO 5428 mile

TOKYO 259 mi 414 Km.

BURBANK 5610 MILES

Death Valley 6116 miles

TOLEDO 6133

DECATUR 9412 M.

SEOUL 34 M. 54 Km.

M*A*S*H
(Bud Gray/MPTV.net)

*M*A*S*H* Signpost, 1970s

Pointing the way to anyplace but here, this prop from *M*A*S*H* (CBS, 1972–1983) reflects the characters' humorous efforts to cope with the horrors of war.

The show, set in an army field hospital during the Korean War, debuted in the final years of the Vietnam War, and its antiwar theme resonated with many Americans. Its talented ensemble cast and compelling storylines earned *M*A*S*H* lasting popularity. The final episode, broadcast on February 28, 1983, was the most watched show in television history.

Right: *Roots* (© Bettmann/CORBIS)

Kunta Kinte's Manacles, 1977

The miniseries *Roots* (ABC, 1977) made television history with its dramatic portrayal of slavery as experienced by several generations of one family.

Based on Alex Haley's autobiographical novel, *Roots* began with Kunta Kinte, an African youth brought to America as a slave in the 1700s, and ended with the emancipation of his descendants during the Civil War. Watched by more than 100 million people, it was a significant departure from programs that had traditionally relegated blacks to minor, stereotyped roles.

SIGNATURE PIECES

Through handcrafted and personalized works of art, individuals express their identity as well as pride in their talents and abilities. These two pieces, made a century apart in different areas of the country, reflect the cultural roots, personal history, and creative vision of their makers. Each tells its own American story.

Table Made by Peter Glass, around 1860

Inlaid with more than 30,000 pieces of wood, this tilt-top center table was created by German immigrant Peter Glass. As a farmer in Wisconsin, Glass applied his native training as a marquetry crafts-man to make award-winning furniture in his spare time.

The elaborate octagonal tabletop combines traditional European designs with patriotic American motifs, including portraits of U.S. military generals. In eight oval plaques encircling the piece, Glass also portrayed himself: "Peter/Glass/Maker/Town/Scott/Wisconsin/U.S. of/America."

"Dave's Dream" Lowrider, 1978–1992

Members of a car club in Chimayó, New Mexico, lovingly transformed this 1969 Ford LTD into a work of art, a memorial, and an expression of community identity and pride.

David Jaramillo began building this lowrider with dreams of winning an auto show trophy, but he died before finishing it. His fam-ily and friends completed "Dave's Dream" as a tribute. With its iridescent paint job, red velour upholstery, and hydraulic suspension system to make it "hop," the car won numerous prizes at lowrider shows.

Victorian House Model, 1876

A masterpiece of craftsmanship, this ornate model was built by Leonard Roth, a Philadelphia shoemaker, and took 10 years to complete.

The house represents the French Second Empire style, which was popular in America from the 1860s to 1880s. It features a double spiral staircase, elaborate gingerbread trim, and mansard roof. With meticulous attention to detail, Roth outfitted the house with windows, a doorbell, and gaslights that actually worked.

Be it a humble bungalow or a sprawling mansion, a house is often the embodiment of the American dream. The Museum's collections include many examples of American houses, both models and life-size. They reflect different ways in which Americans have defined the meaning of home.

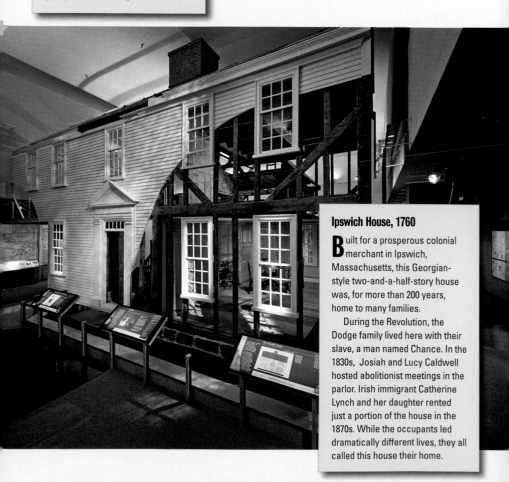

Ipswich House, 1760

B uilt for a prosperous colonial merchant in Ipswich, Massachusetts, this Georgian-style two-and-a-half-story house was, for more than 200 years, home to many families.

During the Revolution, the Dodge family lived here with their slave, a man named Chance. In the 1830s, Josiah and Lucy Caldwell hosted abolitionist meetings in the parlor. Irish immigrant Catherine Lynch and her daughter rented just a portion of the house in the 1870s. While the occupants led dramatically different lives, they all called this house their home.